To Marie,

Peace & Blessings
to you!

PRAISE FOR *A NEW DAY ONE*

"Rodney Walker's story of family and community dysfunction is sad but not unique. I hope his compelling story of triumph will inspire more and more people to offer other young men the kind of intervention and support that a number of wonderful people provided for Rodney. The dividends could be enormous."

—William A. Keyes, president,
The Institute for Responsible Citizenship

"Rodney Walker is one of the top leaders of his generation. Raised in the Chicago foster care system and now a Yale graduate, Rodney has written an honest intelligent and beautiful book that is destined to be an inspirational classic."

—Steve Mariotti, founder,
Network for Teaching Entrepreneurship

"Stories we hear can shape us. Stories we tell about ourselves and our relationships to others can transform us. Rodney Walker's A New Day One *is his story about his life journey that is inspiring. Some people never overcome some of life's harsh realities. Rodney's*

story of how he was and is able to continue to flourish brings us a fresh and empowering understanding of the meaning of new beginnings. As a pastoral theologian and clinical social worker who assists others with how to live a meaningful life particularly after they have experienced traumatic events, A New Day One is a welcomed testimony to our capacity as human beings to endure and thrive."

—Frederick Streets, former chaplain,
Yale University; faculty member, *Yale Divinity School*

"*Rodney Walker is a powerful messenger. His vivid recounting of growing up as an inner-city youth whose life is transformed when given the opportunity to escape a life of poverty teaches us how to dissolve the pipeline to the next generation of poor and homeless Americans.*"

—Judy Cockerton, founder/executive director,
Treehouse Foundation

A NEW

DAY
ONE

A NEW

Trauma, Grace,

and a Young Man's Journey

from Foster Care to Yale

RODNEY J. WALKER

Published by Advantage, Charleston, South Carolina.
Member of Advantage Media Group.

ADVANTAGE is a registered trademark and the Advantage colophon is a trademark of Advantage Media Group, Inc.

Printed in the United States of America.

ISBN: 978-1-59932-745-7
LCCN: 2016930781

This publication is designed to provide accurate and authoritative information in regard to the subject matter covered. It is sold with the understanding that the publisher is not engaged in rendering legal, accounting, or other professional services. If legal advice or other expert assistance is required, the services of a competent professional person should be sought.

Advantage Media Group is proud to be a part of the Tree Neutral® program. Tree Neutral offsets the number of trees consumed in the production and printing of this book by taking proactive steps such as planting trees in direct proportion to the number of trees used to print books. To learn more about Tree Neutral, please visit www.treeneutral.com. To learn more about Advantage's commitment to being a responsible steward of the environment, please visit www.advantagefamily.com/green

Advantage Media Group is a publisher of business, self-improvement, and professional development books and online learning. We help entrepreneurs, business leaders, and professionals share their Stories, Passion, and Knowledge to help others Learn & Grow. Do you have a manuscript or book idea that you would like us to consider for publishing? Please visit advantagefamily.com or call 1.866.775.1696.

To trauma survivors who have not yet recovered,
may this book be the start to your
new day one.

PREFACE

MY PURPOSE, MY DRIVE

The idea to write this book came to me somewhat unexpectedly. I was at the Hudson Theatre in New York, delivering the keynote speech for an entrepreneurship competition. A few years earlier, I had been in the same theater for the same ceremony after winning second place in the national competition, which challenged high school students to create and present a business plan. On this night, however, I found myself on stage telling my story of tragedy and triumph to a crowd of affluent investors, educators, and students, with pictures of South Side clicking by on a projection screen behind me. At the time, I was a junior at Morehouse College and had never thought about writing a book on my life. I was just happy to have made it as far as I had.

After I finished my speech, a woman from the audience approached me looking shaken and excited. She wanted to know more about my story and asked, "Where's your book?" I was caught off guard by her sureness that I would have a book. "I don't have a book," I told her. She smiled and explained that I had only told ten minutes of a whole life's worth of inspiring stories about overcoming adversity. The rest would be equally beneficial, she predicted. Then she said something I still haven't forgotten. "Remember, this may be your calling. If you remember nothing else in life, if I've gotten nothing else from your story, I've gotten this: no one can go back and make a new beginning, but anyone can start today and make a new ending."

I started building on that phrase in my presentations, in my speaking engagements, and even in my personal conversations until it became my most central message as well as my spark for writing this book. We are all more than our past.

ACKNOWLEDGMENTS

I would like to thank and acknowledge Adam Witty and the Advantage Team for both believing in my story and propelling it to a national platform by helping me become a published author. Being an author has long been a dream of mine, and I thank you for seeing the value in my journey. I would like to thank my various mentors for seeing greatness in me at times when I couldn't see it in myself. I appreciate your words of encouragement and affirmation, especially when I lived in an environment surrounded by people who often were negative and discouraging to me. I would like to thank my parents and foster parents for giving me this incredible journey of adversity. Because of you, every student in our nation and the world will know the value of tragedy, pain, despair, and trauma. After reading this book, they will know that their adversity is their greatest asset and that their struggles are preparing them for greatness. I would like to thank every organization, both corporate and nonprofit, that invested in my dreams and taught me the value of investing in myself. Lastly, I would like to thank everyone who continues to follow and invest in me and my commitment to restore the hope, rebuild the dreams, and save the lives of young people all over the world. My continued success is a manifestation of your love and support.

ABOUT THE AUTHOR

Raised in South Side Chicago as a ward of the state from age five, Rodney Walker has become a dynamic entrepreneur, educator, inspirational speaker, and advocate for at-risk youth. Despite his childhood adversity, Walker founded Forever Life Productions, a media company, while still in high school. He holds degrees from Morehouse College and Yale University and travels both nationally and internationally, speaking at educational institutions, corporations, and conferences about the importance of education, entrepreneurship, mentoring, and corporate philanthropy for nonprofit organizations supporting at-risk youth. He has been a guest speaker at events for the Department of Social Services, the Bill & Melinda Gates Foundation, the Clinton Foundation, and the Department of Education and has been a keynote speaker at the White House on the importance of financial literacy for urban youth. Portions of his story have appeared on PBS's *American Graduate Day*, in the documentary *Ten9Eight: Shoot for the Moon*, and in Chelsea Clinton's book, *It's Your World: Get Informed, Get Inspired & Get Going!*

TABLE OF CONTENTS

INTRODUCTION

I knew I had to say something after I left. I was a kid, really, taking off on my first plane ride after eighteen years stuffed inside Chicago's most impoverished South Side pockets. I had gotten into Morehouse College on academic probation—a long shot in the eyes of the admissions department, you could say. I was so accustomed to such assessments that not even the shrinking skyline of the only place I'd ever lived could deter me. No shadow of doubt clouded my mind. No apprehension seized my body. In fact, I remember the excitement vividly, a rush of relief as I watched all I had ever known floating away. There would be real opportunities and a new start in Atlanta, and the vision of whom I wanted to be seemed closer to me now than ever before.

But I still knew that there was more to myself than just me. I hadn't forgotten that. By the time I landed at Hartsfield-Jackson a few hours later, I felt the weight of everyone I knew still roaming the tiny streets, alone in a city that looked so organized and safe from above, pressing down hard on my shoulders.

Where I come from, there's a community of people who have been neglected and mistreated, their children abandoned and abused, and that psychological trauma greatly debilitates their chances for a prosperous future. Most of us never left.

We stayed in the discomfort and struggle because it was familiar, having adapted to an environment that had very little positivity or hope to offer. It's no surprise to me now that youth who are hurt follow the example of other hurt, misguided, and broken individuals in their community, but at the time I couldn't really understand it. Today I see how youth live with distrust for the world because we haven't been afforded opportunities. Given my experience, I understand those feelings in a way few others can. I also understand that a shortage of positive role models leads the youth to find guidance from misguided people with poor intentions for them, and I want to change that. In my own way, I wanted to change it then, too.

As much as my leaving had to do with bettering myself, I knew I wasn't abandoning my peers who remained. Even then, I wanted to encourage them to take that leap of faith, to put down whatever guards they had raised in the face of their adversities and see the possibility of a better life. I wanted to show that it is possible to overcome hardships if we really put our minds to it and learn to let go. I was determined to give my friends and family a story of triumph rather than of trials, tribulations, and tragedy—one that could inspire my neighborhood and spread beyond its borders.

Of course, I had no intention of writing a book at the time; my story of beating the odds was still being written, after all. But after that early flight out of Chicago, one opportunity after another began to present itself to me until

I reached my current place in life, with an opportunity to reflect on the steps that I took.

Through sharing my story of adversity with people across the world, I came to realize that it speaks to a much larger audience than I had ever expected to reach, as everyone has made mistakes, suffered setbacks, had their hearts broken, and even been neglected and abandoned in life in some way, shape, or form. Everyone finds inspiration in a story of never bowing down to whatever difficulties lie before you, but my story is just one out of the millions of inner-city, impoverished youth living in America who still grapple with these circumstances every day, with little direction or help to improve their lives and the communities that raise them. For that reason, I wanted to be their voice, using my whole story to highlight the problems and solutions that exist within these communities.

My beginning is not uncommon. I was born on the South Side of Chicago, living out my youth in some of the city's worst neighborhoods. My mother and father were both raised in Chicago's public housing projects, suffering the same abuse, neglect, and trauma that a life raised by the streets imparts on today's youth. My parents made their mistakes early in life, and by the time my siblings and I were born, they were both struggling with substance abuse and eking out a life in poverty. As a result, my siblings and I spent our childhoods as wards of the State of Illinois, bouncing between relatives, group homes, and foster families for as long as I can remember. Despite my deprived conditions, somehow, someway, I was able to maintain a holistic approach to life and make it through high school, into college, through a top-tier graduate school, into a career in finance, and on to success as an entrepreneur.

All children want to be successful in life; some just begin well behind the starting line and need a specific kind of assistance to overcome their hurdles. People ask me how I overcame my adversities, and the answer isn't as simple as I'd like it to be. At the core, perseverance and humility are the two traits that most helped me achieve my goals, but I didn't pull myself up by the bootstraps one day and charge through my obstacles unassisted. It just doesn't happen that way. I had help. I had mentors, teachers, foundations, family, friends, and people inspired by my efforts that helped me get to where I am today. That's really what made this book possible: the commitment and sacrifice that others made for my future.

But it's also a call to those just like me, the ones who may feel alone and helpless. I hope to be an example that life is full of so much more than the events impacting your life right now, and I hope to educate your sense of normalcy. I want you to know that it's not normal to be living in such harsh and deprived circumstances. It's not normal to see drug addicts on the street corner. It's not normal to see people lined up at the liquor store. It's not normal to be abused and neglected by your parents. It's not normal to be told that you're not worth it. It's not normal to walk out of your house and hear gunfire or to see someone lying dead in the street.

It's not normal to read in the newspaper every day that one of your closest friends or someone you knew was gunned down or went to jail for doing something illegal. This kind of life is not normal, and it isn't your fault. It's an outrage.

In the end, whatever your reality is, it's not what your destiny has to be. We all deserve a new day one.

PROLOGUE

From the early 1900s until the 1970s, the American Southeast experienced the largest wave of internal migration in history. A failed Reconstruction era left the South with a collapsed infrastructure and a particular vulnerability to political corruption, terrorist organizations, and intense economic strife that fueled racial hysteria, Jim Crow laws, and widespread violence.

World War I, World War II, the automobile and oil booms, and a diminished immigrant work force from a war-torn Europe opened hundreds of thousands of manufacturing and labor jobs outside of the South. Expanding and lucrative industries in need of workers willing to work for cheap sought to capitalize on the crisis in the South, and industry representatives were sent to persuade residents to relocate, often needing as little as a one-way bus ticket to recruit them. Alongside more than eleven million white Southerners and one million Latino Southerners, roughly seven million black Southerners left their homes for the Midwest, West Coast, and Northeast in what is known today as the Southern Diaspora.

The migration spread Evangelicalism, particularly such Protestant faiths as Baptist, Methodism, Pentecostalism, and

Presbyterianism; music like rock 'n' roll, blues, jazz, country, bluegrass, R&B, and gospel; Southern culinary traditions; and a large working-class labor force desperate for jobs and housing.

As migrants relocated, a large and equally desperate European immigrant population and native working class rose in opposition to the influx of competitors. Italian and Irish gangs formed to both combat the migrants and secure their newly adopted communities and socioeconomic interests. Before long, ethnicities began to blend and racial lines became more distinguishable.

In South Side Chicago, thousands of black Americans settled in the Bronzeville borough, establishing their own street organizations for protection as well as their own small businesses, schools, and community organizations during a time of legal social segregation across the country. As European immigrants and white Americans experienced both greater upward social mobility and a desire to move out of black-dominated neighborhoods, much of South Side began to see the establishment of a majority black population. The Irish and Italian gangs largely dissolved after the end of the prohibition era, and the immigrants they depended on began to integrate over generations. But for most black Americans, integration was stalled due to societal racism. As a result, gangs became more ingrained in the communities, policies ignorant of their problems failed, and racial divisions began to calcify.

After the Civil Rights movement desegregated the nation, more opportunities opened for black Americans, and those already in the middle class and those who could secure higher-paying jobs moved into neighborhoods with better schools, hospitals, and facilities. As the money left, black-owned businesses closed in large numbers, leaving behind working-class and poor black residents with increasingly underfunded schools and public facilities. Discrimination against loan seekers with low incomes compounded problems until the Community Reinvestment Act—part of the Housing and Community Development Act of 1977—helped alleviate the problems. But government policies, whether purposely or negligently, had already systemically begun tearing down the community and enforcing the confinement of black Americans, allowing for generational poverty and its respective trauma to flourish. The continued lack of opportunities led to a deep sense of distrust for the system of government as a whole—a system that poor communities were now dependent on for housing, food, medical care, and other basic living expenses.

By the end, systemic and social barriers had greatly disabled the inner-city black community by blocking the avenues for upward mobility. Fears, violence, and neglect gave rise to street organizations, which created a cycle of survival that depended on drug trafficking and ignited a substance abuse problem among segments of these communities. The ensuing War on Drugs removed large swaths of black men from the community, hardening them in prison, stripping their right to vote, and making it even more difficult for them to gain legitimate employment. Children grew up traumatized and without positive male role models, a cycle that continues today across much of South Side and beyond.

CHAPTER
ONE

CAST AWAY

Rodney and his younger sister, Samantha, in 1998.
This was their final visit before being separated for ten years.

"How are you liking where you're staying?" I remember Victoria, a social worker and counselor, ask me.

I shrugged, looking down to my fingers pulling at my shirtsleeve. "It's fine I guess."

"Okay, well, how is the transition going? Do you feel safe at your new home?"

"It's fine. . . Really, though, I want to know when I'll be able to see my parents again. When do I go home?"

"I'm sorry, but I don't know the answer to that, Rodney."

"How come I can't see them now? How come I can't just see them today?"

"It's more complicated than that, Rodney. Do you know how many foster homes you've been in since we first started having these talks? Can you tell me how many times you've moved up to this point?"

I thought as hard as I could, flipping through the different beds, rooms, faces, streets—everything I could remember about my foster homes, but I couldn't be sure of how many there had been in total. "I don't know," I said, defeated, my eyes returning to my fingers.

"You've been relocated twelve different times over the last six or seven years, Rodney. We have twelve different addresses for you on file, which makes your going home more . . . involved. You've primarily been living with your relatives, which is why your parents were still seeing you whenever they wanted. But now that you're living with a nonrelative foster parent, that's just not possible. It just can't happen like that anymore."

I was eleven years old at the time, six years after being officially placed into foster care, and it was the first time I realized my life was not normal. It was the first session out of more than sixty in which an adult explained it to me in blunt terms: "You don't belong to your parents anymore."

THE SHATTERED FRAGMENTS

We were not afraid, my brothers and I. There was no panic in our voices, no pacing or crying or screaming. I was four years old, believing everything was fine and normal. We would be going home soon. *The Cosby Show* would be on, and my brothers and I would lie on our elbows between the toes of our mother and father and watch the Huxtables negotiate comedic plights of life in wealthy Brooklyn Heights. By the time the credits rolled, my brothers and I would be out cold, and my father would drape us two at a time over his narrow shoulders, laying us down softly on the mattress we shared with the rest of my siblings in the back room. But for now, we just needed to wait a little longer while our parents reconciled with the courts.

Everything comes in shattered fragments after that. Like a car crash: ears ringing, hands shaking, muffled screams. There was yelling and cursing and crying from the adults—the panic setting in now. My youngest brother, my youngest sister, and I arrived on 63rd and King Drive, outside a woman's house we would come to call "Big Ma." She wasn't any relation to us, and to this day I'm not sure how we knew her, but we stayed with her for a few months while our parents fought in court to regain custody of us. I was too young for any of it to make sense. In my mind, we were just sleeping over someplace until my parents came to pick us up.

When I moved in with my father's mother, my grandmother, I was separated from my younger brother and sister and joined my two older brothers, who were six and eight years old at the time. I didn't learn until much later that they, along with my other siblings under the age of eighteen, had been placed with relatives or foster families scattered around Chicago.

The fragments begin to merge in my mind, as my mother and father would stay with us at my grandmother's regularly and offer us visions of normalcy. Although we were in foster care, the only times I realized that fact was when my siblings and I would have to meet at the Department of Children and Family Services for what was called "parent-children meetings." These were monthly sessions in which children in foster homes, like some of my siblings, would have an opportunity to see their parents. I didn't grasp the trauma my siblings must have been experiencing at the time. To me, our parents had not gone anywhere. No paperwork or people with name tags ever came between us. The only thing different was their periodic absence and the fact that we were staying at Grandmother's house instead of our own.

My father had begun taking courses at Malcolm X College on Chicago's West Side, and he would stay with us almost nightly, watching movies with us and tucking us in before we fell asleep. He would take us to the park down the street nearly every other day, and on some weekends, we would all go out to my grandmother's favorite restaurant, a Hyde Park diner called Mellow Yellow.

My mother would be there most days, too, helping to care for my grandmother and making sure we got up on time and were dressed for school. I developed a close relationship with her during this time, and I can recall vividly how much she loved to talk. We spent hours just talking about anything and everything. She would correct us on our grammar, telling us not to use words like "ain't" and to say "yes" instead of "yeah." She taught us English words that we didn't learn in school, and when one of us did well on a test or brought home a good report card, she would always congratulate us and make sure we knew that she was proud of us. When I didn't get good grades, my teachers would sometimes tell her that I was "remedial" and had learning problems, but she would just shake her head, look them in the eyes, and say confidently, "He is not slow. Hear me?" She was my best advocate even then, and I remember her as a really great mother, full of love and the nurturing instincts she had first developed while looking after her younger siblings as a preteen and on.

We would be with my parents for the summers, too. My mom would take us to Bloomington, Illinois, during summer breaks, and later she got an apartment in the Cabrini-Green housing projects, where we lived with her for a few months. Sometimes we would visit my aunt Ernestine and would stay with her from time to time when my mom couldn't be home.

Unfortunately, being a good mother and a good father didn't necessarily make them good parents, especially in the eyes of social services. I was too young to understand what was keeping us from going home, and the comfortability my grandmother and other relatives gave us allowed my brothers and me to not really care all that much. But as months turned into years and we still weren't all home together again, I was growing more and more curious about what was going on.

By the time I was in the third grade, my brothers and I had moved in with my dad's sister a neighborhood away from my grandmother. We kept roughly the same schedule and lifestyle we had grown accustomed to at my grandmother's house. My parents spent most nights there with us, and we went to the same school, parks, and other places—everything was almost exactly as it had been.

After a series of disagreements began to fester between my mother and aunt, none of which I can remember distinctly, my brother Vincent and I moved again, this time to my cousin's house across town in Bellwood, Illinois.

Still, nothing triggered in my mind that anything was wrong. My parents were still involved and visiting us often, my brothers and I were still near one another, and we were always surrounded by family. It was just another move and nothing more, really. I never asked my parents why we moved from place to place. In fact, it never even crossed my mind to ask. Looking back, I know the reason I never had the impulse to ask was because I moved around so much at an early age and just thought it was normal, something that everyone did. I became used to social workers telling me, "Things have changed. You have to move. Something has happened, and you have to move. We have another living situation for you. We need you to pack your things." Kids haven't experienced enough to know when an experience is abnormal, so I remember just doing as I was told by gathering my things, filling my backpack and suitcase with clothes and a few toys, and riding quietly to another house.

It wasn't until Vincent and I arrived at another cousin's house about a year later that I began to grow restless and act out. I had just turned ten years old and had become so used to being able to pack up and leave that when my cousin disciplined us for not following her rules, I refused to stay. It was the first time I ever made the decision to move, and it was as simple as me saying to my social worker, "I'm not happy. I want to leave." And like some magical command, I was whisked away to another home. I remember the excitement I felt that first time, a sense of power in an otherwise powerless situation, and I rushed to pack my bags when the social worker arrived to pick me up. I didn't think about where I was going. I didn't think about what this move really meant. I didn't think about the fact that I was leaving Vincent, even as he cried and said he didn't want me to go. What I was doing just didn't register with me. I never thought about the long-term effects that leaving the care of relatives would have and how leaving their care would cost me the daily access to my parents. I didn't understand my parents' strategy for getting around the system at all. I was just happy to leave because I didn't want to be there anymore. Simple as that.

I arrived at the Mercy Home for Boys and Girls, a group home for foster children in Chicago's West Loop, a few minutes later. After I was checked in by the social workers and settled into a room, I was given a long rundown of the rules by one of the workers. Until I could be placed into a more permanent foster home, I would wake up at 8:00 a.m., wash up, play outside for an hour, watch a movie indoors for two hours, have a group activity with the other kids, and then shower before lights-out.

The boys campus was large and divided into nine homes, each housing roughly ten boys. I was in a home for boys between the ages of eleven and fourteen, and while I saw frequent fights between some of the boys who were extremely distraught, I was never a target of abuse.

All in all, my time at the Mercy Home was brief, only a period of four or five weeks, and relatively calm. But it was there that I started to realize the reality of my life was not exactly normal. I began to withdraw from social activities, became introverted and shy, and started to see how unhappy I was becoming over my situation. It was an awakening of sorts, in that I was old enough to grasp my emotional state and see that my condition was not well.

Around the same time, a lady that my younger brother, Aaron, had lived with learned about my situation. She contacted her sister, who agreed to take me in for a while. I was moved from the Mercy Home to her house shortly afterward, and I lived with her for about a month before moving to a temporary foster home. Temporary foster homes were fairly common, as most foster caretakers operate on a kind of rotation schedule, taking kids in for short periods of time while social services search for a foster "parent," which is basically someone who wants to take them in permanently.

Afterward, I relocated to two temporary placement homes before moving to my last foster home. In my mind, I was playing a horrible game. "Just keep playing," I would think to myself. "Social services will get tired of keeping me away from my parents, foster homes will stop offering to take me in, and eventually I'll wear everyone down enough that they'll give up and take me home." All I had to do was keep calling the social workers with complaints and wait. "It will all be over soon."

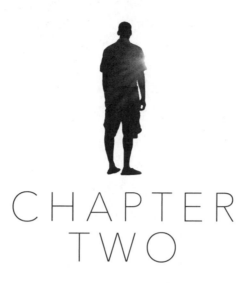

CHAPTER TWO

AROUND THE CORNER, OUT OF THE WAY

At eleven years old, I was moved to a long-stay foster home. Coincidentally, my new home was only a couple of neighborhoods away from my real home, with my parents no more than a few miles away. But despite being so close, I never felt farther away. And once a permanent foster home was found, the chances of my parents regaining custody dwindled to near extinction. I was beginning to understand the futility of my struggle to get home in a way I never had before.

My new home consisted of my foster mother and her two daughters. Like my previous foster homes, there was no father present, which seemed to be the most common situation within the foster care system: single mothers, whose main skill was caring for children—changing diapers, cooking, maintaining bedtimes, and seeing to it that we got to and from school every day. Not that being a mother is an easy job, far from it, but one of its most difficult and important tasks is centered on making children feel loved and valued. In some of my previous foster care experiences, neglected children seemed to be regarded as more of a commodity or a chore rather than individuals to raise and love. You were housed, fed, and clothed, but there was no real relationship to develop. There were no life lessons, very little affection, and no moments of togetherness laughing and talking as a family, because we knew we weren't really a family. It was an arrangement that decently served our present situations and nothing more.

In the beginning, I was very comfortable at my last home. My foster mother was a really great parent, and her daughters were really great siblings. But we really didn't know what we were getting ourselves into. She couldn't have known that I didn't want to be anywhere but with my family. And I couldn't have known that she was looking for the son she never had.

I came into her life through a family relative who told her I was in foster care and needed a permanent home. She took me in with loving intentions and was great at keeping me out of trouble and ensuring that I had structure in my life, but a disconnect started when I decided that I didn't want to be there anymore. From the beginning, I was still bewildered about why I couldn't get home, and we had frequent disagreements because of it.

I think under any other circumstance, in any other foster home, I could have easily left. I'd had problems with foster parents before, and even for the smallest disagreements, I could leave without a problem. I'd just say I wanted to leave, call the social worker, and I would be taken away. This situation was different because the social workers had grown tired, or perhaps just doubtful, of my calls to be moved. They met every call I made with responses meant to discourage me from trying to go home, saying things like, "You might not want to do this. Make this work because there's no telling where you're going to end up. You could wind up in a group home with some very bad kids. It's too dangerous. It's too unstable for you to move now. Make it work here."

The social workers knew I had no chance of going home, and they also knew the sad reality that because I had been moved so many times and was getting older, I was no longer easy to place. While they were right, all I understood was that I was being told I couldn't go home. What began as a sleepover at my grandmother's was turning into a two-thousand-night sleepover with strangers. I was already exhausted and homesick, and now I felt that I was losing any freedom I'd had to leave a place where I wasn't comfortable.

Along with a more permanent foster home came more separation from my parents. I was not given an opportunity to visit them whenever I wanted or however much I wanted. Of course, there were reasons for the restrictions, such as my parents' battle with addiction and legal troubles, but I was unaware of their struggles and believed that my social workers and foster mother were trying to take me away from them. I envisioned my parents searching for me, combing through the streets calling out my name, fighting tooth and nail in the courts to bring my siblings and me back home. If there was ever a time that I reached the depths of yearning for my family, it was then, during those first few months with my foster family. Every bit of me felt it—a burning deep within me to find my brothers and sisters and get back to my parents.

Once I realized that I only wanted to be with my family, I didn't want any other. No alternative would satisfy me. But I was running out of options to reunite with them, and that's when things really went downhill. I grew more introverted and more frustrated, my grades began to suffer, and feelings of hopelessness and loneliness became constants in my life.

I spent days locked in my bedroom, listening to music all day and night, trying to forget about what was happening in my own life. During the summers, I wouldn't go outside and play. I didn't have any friends, so I slept most of the day and all night unless I absolutely had to get out of bed. If I had to get up to wash the dishes or do laundry, I would do it. If I had to go with my foster parent to one of her relative's houses, I would go. If I had to go on a vacation trip with my foster family, I would try to have fun, but I wasn't excited or enthused to go. I just wanted to be by myself.

The idea of having to be somewhere I really didn't want to be left me feeling extremely stressed and depressed. I remember saying to myself all the time, "I can't wait until I turn eighteen. Then I can do what I want to do. I don't have to be anywhere I don't want to be. I can just go." I couldn't escape my situation, which killed me in a lot of ways. I felt trapped, and my sense of creativity, ambition, confidence, and comfort slowly melted away.

NEW JOURNEY, OLD PROBLEMS

When I graduated from eighth grade, I applied to high schools late and wasn't eligible to go to any except my neighborhood school, Wendell Phillips Academy. At the time, Wendell Phillips Academy was one of the worst high schools in the city of Chicago, listed among the most violent in South Side. In the year I entered high school, Phillips and Orr High School, on the West Side, had two of the highest dropout rates in all of the Chicago metro area.

I remember my foster mom being nervous about me going to Phillips because she knew how violent and gang affiliated it had become. When she found out about a charter school that was starting up that year, she applied immediately. ACE (Architecture, Construction, and Engineering) Technical Charter High School was set to launch its first year and hosted an open house for families to attend and learn more information. Admission was on a first-come, first-served basis, and I was the seventh person to apply. Because she acted so quickly, I got in. Only 150 students entered the school that year, making me one of only a relative handful that received such a good opportunity.

Despite the opportunity at school, life at home was a growing challenge. The psychological abuse of my situation became more apparent to me as I got older. A lack of control over anything in my life left me feeling like a prisoner most days, especially when my family needed me.

My grandmother became severely ill in the early 2000s and was admitted to a nursing home for the last few years of her life. Having found where I was, my father came by with the rest of my brothers to pick me up and take me to visit her. I remember my father standing in the front yard, saying to my foster mother that my grandmother had Alzheimer's.

"She's sick," he said. "We don't know how long she's going to be here. We want to know if Rodney can come."

"No," she told him. "He didn't wash the dishes. He can't go."

My father and brothers had no choice but to leave without me.

That stayed with me. It affected me deeply because I no longer felt like I was allowed to be a part of my family even under the gravest of circumstances. My grandmother passed away a few months later. After I attended her funeral, I wanted to leave more than ever.

High school was the best environment for me at that time, but even there, I struggled to find a place where I belonged. I was dealing with the problem of being somewhere I didn't want to be, and everything that happened in the house carried over into school. I was emotionally distraught, which left me with very low self-esteem. I didn't communicate very well with other students and spent most of my high school years as an introvert. As a result, my grades suffered for the first couple of years, I didn't have any friend groups, and I really struggled in a lot of ways, both socially and academically.

I joined the basketball team during my freshman year. I was in need of somewhere to release all the emotions I had in me, and basketball, which I liked, was available to me. But I never found a sense of belonging there. I wasn't a good basketball player, and because I wasn't, it never fueled my passion or gave me an outlet for all that energy.

I joined the robotics club and the chess team. I also joined the first tennis and softball teams my school had. I was a part of all these activities I had no interest in or passion for only because I needed to do something besides staying in the house, being somewhere I didn't want to be. So, whatever activity I could find that allowed me to stay after school, I did it.

Unfortunately, all the activities and emotional distress took their toll on my grades, and by the time of my first progress report, I had three Fs, two Cs, and a D—amounting to a 1.3 GPA. My basketball coach (and school dean), Mr. Coleman, saw my progress report and said, "You got three

Fs on your progress report. There's no way you can play with these grades. I don't understand how you can make these grades. I just don't understand. If you want to play basketball, you can't play for this team. We don't accept these types of grades."

I really wanted to remain on the basketball team, so I made every effort to make good grades. On the next progress report, I turned all those Fs into Cs and was able to play, but Mr. Coleman knew there was more going on. He had a history of working to be involved in the personal lives of his players and students as much as possible. In my sophomore year, I got into a nasty argument with my foster mom and was called to meet with Mr. Coleman. When I arrived at his office, I found my foster mom seated and ready to talk about it.

Mr. Coleman asked, "What's going on? What's the problem? He's making terrible grades. How can we fix this?"

My foster mom spoke first and told him, "Rodney has been disrespectful. He's not doing what I tell him to do. He's not doing his chores. He doesn't listen. I don't know why he's not doing well at school. He gets treated well, but he's ungrateful. I don't know why he acts the way he does."

I told my coach, "That's not true. I just feel like I want to be with my parents. I want to visit more often. My grandmother just passed, and I wasn't even able to go see her before she passed. She told me it was because I didn't wash the dishes, and I got upset."

At the time, my coach took the side of my foster mom. That really hurt my feelings, so I ran out of the office and said there was no way I could stay in her home. He told me he understood what I was going through but that I needed to pull myself together and do my best to deal with it because there was nothing I could do about my situation. I knew he was right, but again I felt that my struggle was being dismissed and that there was no hope for living with my family again. I would just have to endure it.

A SOUTH SIDE SOCIETY

There was a silver lining to my introversion, one that constructed a wall between the streets and me, keeping the gangs, dope dealers, pimps, and other environmental pitfalls out of my path. By nature, I didn't like to be around groups of people, so I inherently avoided slipping in with the wrong crowd.

In impoverished environments like South Side, you have to find where you fit in or else someone will find where to put you. Aside from my reserved nature, I was fortunate enough to have foster parents and teachers who were really good at monitoring my outside social life.

The people I associated with on the South Side were kids who generally had the same types of experiences I had growing up in foster care, only they weren't in foster care. Every child on the South Side who grew up in the communities where I grew up, mainly Bronzeville and Englewood, had the same memories of a certain culture of discipline, both good and bad. If we did something wrong, we got beat with the same belts, the same extension cords, the same fists and hands. And most of us snuck out sometimes and ran the streets when our parents were away doing whatever they were doing.

In fact, the few friends that I had grew up in situations that were a lot worse than mine. Like me, most didn't have a father present all the time and would often be disrespectful toward their moms. That was a common theme on the South Side—a lot of single mothers raising their kids. In the areas of Chicago where I grew up, you could see how much the drug trade and the related antidrug campaign on poor communities of color affected the area by the number of single moms.

Most of our parents were on drugs, suffering from crack cocaine and heroin addiction. My friends and I used to make jokes about how bad it was to be a crackhead. We would call each other crackheads when we were insulting each other and talk about using and selling drugs, although we never really did.

Because there was no leadership, especially black male leadership, a lot of kids got into trouble. There were a lot of young mothers on the South Side, as there still are today, and the adults couldn't control the youth. Kids looking to belong somewhere ran with groups of kids, usually getting into trouble when parents couldn't keep tabs on them.

By and large, our community was made up of young boys and girls like me who felt like our biggest influence came from each other because we didn't have any strong males around to guide us. I felt safe at school with my peers, and as a result my social life revolved around extracurricular activities after school. When I had to be home, I would pass the time alone in my room listening to music I recorded off the radio onto cassette tapes.

Eventually, when my frustrations boiled over, I began lashing out. My foster mother and I started having frequent disagreements over things most families probably experience, such as not cleaning up when I was supposed to, not checking in, getting into silly arguments with her daughters, and saying things I shouldn't have. The disagreements began to escalate into physical reprimands, as her attempts to bring me under control grew more desperate.

But none of those things destroyed our relationship or completely snapped my spirit. To me, what really broke our relationship was that my heart did not belong there, and my mind was set to resist everything about it. I wanted to go back home and be with my own family, and I was tired of being told that I couldn't.

It wouldn't be the last time that the unfortunate reality I had tumbled into confronted me so clearly. When I was fourteen, I wrote a letter to my foster mother telling her I didn't want to live with her anymore, that I didn't like being forced to be somewhere I didn't want to be. Not long after I gave her my letter, a social worker came to the house to talk to me. She sat me down, and after some attempts to change my mind, a seriousness overtook her voice. "If you leave this foster home, no one is going to take you. Nobody is going to want you. You're fourteen years old. No one is going to want to take you at this age because you're coming from a lot of foster homes. That looks bad to foster parents. Nobody wants to deal with that. You're either going to make it work here, or you might go to a place that's a lot worse. Trust me, you don't want to go to a group home permanently. It's going to be abusive. There are kids in there who've been in a lot of trouble. You'll go through a lot of hard times if you go there. You'd be better off staying here and dealing with this situation."

At that point, I felt I didn't have any power over my situation. Even my social worker didn't want to help me anymore. I felt more helpless, lost, and alone than ever before.

RUNAWAY

The distance between my foster mother and me continued to expand as I got older, and by the time I was seventeen, I was sneaking out to visit my parents every chance I got. At times it felt like I was living in some alternate universe, escaping a prison camp to spend a few fleeting hours with my mother and father, peeling back tiny pieces of the lives we had lost.

Over the course of several weeks, these visits caused verbal altercations with my foster mother to spiral. One night, I was confronted at my parents' house and escorted out by the police. It was a very traumatic event. I had never been in a police car—at least not that I can remember. After I was returned to my foster mother, I said to myself over and over, "I'm going to run away. I'm going to run away for good. I'll go back to my parents' house and hide, and everything will be okay." While I knew I wanted to make a break for it, I had no idea when or how I would do it.

The next morning I went to school and sat through a day's worth of classwork agonizing over what to do. Early on, I convinced myself that I wasn't going to take the 29 State Street bus back to 46th Street to my foster home. Instead, I kept repeating to myself, "I'm going to run away. I'm not going back."

I was really nervous about it because I knew my parents could get into serious trouble for having me there again. I played back what the police had told my parents over and over in my head in a loop: "Don't have him come back here. He's not in your custody. You could get arrested, and she could take legal action against you." Nevertheless, I decided to run away and deal with whatever happened.

That afternoon, I went to my parents' house on 52nd and Princeton, showing up at the door unannounced. My father answered. "What are you doing?" he asked, confused. "Is she with you?"

"No," I told him. "I just came by myself. I didn't go home. I decided to come here."

We talked, and I remember him telling me, "You can't stay here. You know the police are going to come over here again. She can send them back over here, and we can get in trouble."

My mom came home later and called her sister. "Rodney is over here," she told her. "I need you to keep him for a little while." My aunt came over later on that day to pick me up, and I ended up staying at her house for a few days. The next morning, the police showed up at my parents' door and searched the house, only to discover that I wasn't there. They asked my parents if they knew where I was, but of course, they told them no. The police told my parents that I was missing and that they would let them know if they found out where I was.

Meanwhile, my aunt kept quiet, and I stayed at her house. I was out of school, and I didn't communicate with anybody except my parents while I was staying there.

Then my foster mother decided to end the search. She called my parents and said, "I know you all know where he is. I know he's over there. I just want to let you all know I'm not fighting this anymore. You can keep him. Tell him he can come over to my apartment and get his clothes and all his stuff, all his things." I could leave and never go back again.

My parents called and let her know I would be over to get my things the next day, but I was nervous to go back. I didn't know what to expect by confronting her. "What will she say to me? What will I say?" I kept thinking to myself. I knew that her feelings were hurt. I knew that everything she had done, she had done because she was hurt. She didn't do it out of spite. She was, in a way, heartbroken. But my desire to be with my family was much deeper, and I was ready to get home by any means necessary.

The next day, I waited until nightfall to make the trip over. My dad drove me to her apartment, and I slowly walked to the gate and rang the doorbell. She buzzed me in, and I walked in the gate. I walked up the stairs, and when I got to the door, my clothes were in suitcases outside the door. I never actually saw her face. I just saw my clothes. I picked them up, ran down the stairs, out of the gate, into my dad's car, and we left. Within minutes, twelve years of struggling to break free was over.

When I got my clothes and we got back to the house, I felt like a weight had been lifted off my shoulders. I felt like I didn't have to run anymore. I didn't have to worry about the police coming to get me. I didn't have to go back to a home where I didn't want to be, and I was no longer under the control of someone other than my parents. I didn't have to deal with all the tension that was there. I felt a great burden lift off my shoulders, and a sense of joy rose up in me. And because of that joy and the sense that my determination for something good had finally paid off, the power of perseverance and hope flourished in my mind, and my life started to turn in the right direction.

A week after I left my foster mother's house permanently, she showed up at my school's office. I was in math class when I heard a voice over the intercom say, "Rodney Walker, please report to the office."

I went to the office, and she was sitting in one of the seats right in front of me as soon as I walked in. She didn't stand; instead, she just said calmly, "Here, I want you to write an agreement down for me on this piece of paper." Then she handed me a pen and a white piece of paper. I don't remember everything I wrote, but it was to the effect that I was no longer under her custody as of that day. I had to write down the date, that I was seventeen years old, and that all relationships with us would cease beyond that day. Then she signed it and left. I was no longer under her custody, and I officially moved in with my parents.

CHAPTER
THREE

TRACING THE FRACTURE

I n Chicago, most children come into foster care though the Department of Children and Family Services, and parents have a narrow window to regain custody. Once the family is broken, parents have specific things they need to do before they can regain their parental rights and reclaim guardianship of their children.

One of the first breaking points in my family came when my dad was arrested and we were separated in foster care. That was the first step, but recovery was still possible. My parents had chances to successfully complete their court proceedings, parental classes, and rehabilitation for substance abuse. They had visitation meetings where they needed to visit with us every week or so, and they had to complete these mandates in order to get us back.

Emotionally, my mother couldn't maintain her composure while this process was going on. She'd tell me it felt like rape to see social workers take her kids away and then tell her to do all these tricks to get us back.

It was very emotional for her because she felt the system was dangling us from a leash, asking her how badly she wanted her kids. What the system called a comprehensive rehabilitation and reintegration program turned out to have unintended consequences. A result of my mother's addictions and childhood traumas, she was already emotionally unstable and just couldn't handle losing her kids, too. Ultimately, this sent her deeper into depression and substance abuse.

Whenever she went to court, she would lash out in anger and storm out of the courtroom. She was uncooperative with rules and often unresponsive to the court instructions and requirements. Sometimes she didn't come to visitation, so they would mark that against her and say, "This shows how much of an unstable parent she is." As a result, my mom permanently lost custody of us early on.

My dad, on the other hand, was more cooperative. He was able to maintain his composure and go to the meetings, go to the visitations, and take the required classes, but his lifestyle eventually caught up to him when he was arrested and charged with possession of a controlled substance with the intent to sell. Once he was arrested, it was effectively the end of my parents' chances for getting us back.

I was eager to learn everything that had been going on. I wanted to know why we were in this terrible world, scattered across Chicago, living like strangers that used to be a family. I wanted to know why our reintegration was such a failure, and I wanted to know where my brothers and sisters were. My parents were only able to keep a close relationship with three of the seven children who went into foster care. My younger siblings either were adopted or sank too deeply into the system and drifted away from my parents.

Aside from that, I learned very little. I knew there were things they were still hiding from me, and a part of me wanted to live without knowing. I wanted to allow myself the peace of slipping into comfortable ignorance, believing it was all some tragic mistake or evil act perpetrated by institutional and societal racism, but I couldn't keep myself from wanting more answers. I asked "Why?" incessantly—whenever they gave me small and short answers instead of the long and complicated ones I knew I deserved.

In the beginning, my parents skirted a lot of the specifics about how and why my siblings and I were taken away, but as I got older they began to lay out the longer history of their present lives. What I was ultimately asking them was: Why did you fail me as a parent? For this, there was no simple answer—no answer that I would be able to understand at seventeen years old anyway—so they answered my question by giving me more questions to ask, revealing more depth in their lives for me to sift through. As I listened, I began to make sense of the horrible conclusion their choices had brought on, understanding that behind every story is another story.

THE PAST'S PRESENT

Sometime during the 1940s, my maternal grandmother and her family left Arkansas for Chicago, and some of my father's family packed up and fled New Orleans, all taking part in the Great Migration of southerners seeking better economic opportunity, civic engagement, and broader racial equality. The reality wasn't quite the utopia that the figurative brochure had promised, but both families did find a vibrant black community in South Side during that time.

As time went on, discriminatory policies and practices greatly stunted South Side's growth and stability, and the Civil Rights movement was beginning to change the inner-city landscape, for better and for worse. By the time my parents were entering their teens, generational poverty, childhood neglect and abuse, drug addiction and alcoholism, and societal tensions were wreaking a devastating psychological toll on the South Side society.

My mother was molested when she was eleven years old. Perhaps worst of all, it was by her father, who had just come back into her life after leaving shortly after her birth. Almost immediately after she first met him, he began abusing her, until he left again six months later. She told me that one time he beat her so badly that she couldn't feel the bottom half of her body and had to be taken to the emergency room.

Before the age of twelve, my mother was mostly estranged from her mother, who spent nearly all of her time working and going to school, and she was the primary caretaker for her younger siblings. She began partying with friends and running the project streets and hanging out with the wrong type of people. She was exposed to that lifestyle at an early age, did drugs at an early age, and lived through the trauma of both her best friend and her brother being brutally murdered. She became pregnant and had her first child at thirteen, which forced her to abandon her education altogether. From the very beginning, my mother's life was in crisis.

My father also grew up without his father present, but unlike my mother's experience, his mother was loving and tried to be as present as possible. She worked nights as a bartender, however, and my father would skip school some days to hang out all night with his friends while his mother worked. Nights out in the housing project often led to all types of trouble, and the last thing he and his friends were thinking about was the responsibility of school.

With no strong male leadership and a working mother, most kids have to prioritize things on their own somehow, some way. In an impoverished community, parents have to focus on the economics of life first and foremost. Their concerns center on the essentials, like paying rent and making sure the family has enough money for groceries and other necessities. Making sure that their kids are in school on a day-to-day basis and getting good grades just isn't the top priority. My parents didn't have that support, and as a result, neither of them made it through high school.

As a byproduct of fatherlessness, negative peer influence, and the socioeconomic conditions in the urban public housing projects, both of my parents were exposed to drugs at an early age. My mom started smoking cigarettes as early as nine years old, and my dad started smoking as early as eleven or twelve. They were both exposed to marijuana before they were teenagers. This was common for most urban inner-city youth growing up in conditions of poverty.

My father was raised in the Harold Ickes Homes and my mother in Cabrini-Green. Both housing projects were among the more violent housing projects of that time and were demolished in the late 1990s and 2000s due to the crime and condemnable living conditions.

While my mother entered motherhood early and turned to the streets for her survival and coping mechanisms, my father joined the Marines and served in Vietnam. He would tell stories about some of his experiences there, recalling the horror in vivid detail to this day. Like so many others, he developed a heroin addiction in Vietnam as he attempted to cope with the trauma of war.

My father's return to the States fit a common pattern for Vietnam veterans in South Side. He bounced around low-income jobs, dabbled in petty crime as he battled his addiction and PTSD, and eventually developed a criminal record. It made the reintegration even worse that veterans were coming home not only to poverty but also to an outright gunning down of their community, with the assassination or imprisonment of the most prominent civil rights leaders of the era. By the end of the sixties, the shots meant to silence the hope in humanity seemed to have found their mark, and the seeds of a decades-long struggle sprouted from the shells.

FROM WASTELAND TO GANGLAND

Rodney's uncle, Cedrick Maltbia, was a major Chicago gang leader until he was murdered in 1981 at the age of twenty-four.

With the experience in organizational leadership and weapons training they gained from Vietnam, in the sixties and seventies, black men in South Side began to form "community organizations" to help secure their neighborhoods and support the residents economically.

These groups weren't all bad. In fact, they did a lot of good for their communities in the beginning. They held food drives every month and brought in truckloads of turkey and chicken during the holidays to feed the community. They established basketball, football, and other sports leagues for the kids, offering them something positive to put their energy into. They had members make sure women got home safely at night. Leaders looked out for the children in the community so they would not involve themselves in fighting. They had peace zones where people could come together and socialize without violence. They organized concerts, block parties, and other activities for the community as well.

This was all basically controlled chaos, and businesses and residents were expected to pay a fee in exchange for the services and protection that the government was not providing. The way they saw it, these street organizations were the guardians of the community. They would relay a message to businesses and residents, "Why are you paying taxes to an establishment that doesn't care about protecting you or keeping your streets clean? They don't care if you have food and water on the table or if you have jobs. You're paying taxes to an establishment that does not make sure any of this is happening for us, so why not support an organization that can really keep you safe?"

During the second half of the twentieth century, Chicago gave rise to more than one hundred minority street and political organizations across the city—most notably the Illinois chapter of Black Panther Party, the Black Gangster Disciple Nation, the Black P. Stone Nation, and the Vice Lords. Like many poor and disadvantaged families, some of my elders and relatives became involved in street organizations in their childhood years. My mother's brother, Bo, was one of the most known among them, having amassed a reputation on the streets as a high-ranking member prior to his murder at twenty-four years of age. In spite of the violence, it's understandable how these social groups were so attractive to young, energetic men who were living with depravity and neglect. They provided an outlet for young people when the world failed to open its doors to them.

Failed socioeconomic policies, the distrust for government and law enforcement, and a rebellious, disenfranchised culture made street organizations like the Stones and Disciples a mainstay in the black community. Government officials had jurisdiction over these communities, but the residents were not their priority for a number of reasons—the community had no political voice or representation, did not make up a large percentage of votes, and did not fit the political or economic interest of most officials.

Among all the other variables, the aggressive drug and crime campaigns from the seventies to the present day ultimately broke the back of impoverished black communities like South Side. It was during the seventies that employment, banking, and housing discrimination were still palpable across the country. Whether based on racism or low incomes, housing loans in predominantly black neighborhoods were often nonexistent or attached to high interest rates and fees.

Just as communities were built in the city, communities were also being built in the jails. These universities of crime and violence began churning out thousands of violent, gang-affiliated men who built legions of followers. They knew they wouldn't be able to maintain a steady, legitimate job because of their criminal background, so they came out looking to make their money in other ways. With felony records, hardened dispositions, and a lack of opportunities, the communities in the jails moved into the neighborhoods looking to get right into the business of survival in whatever ways they had to.

Like my Uncle Bo—as kids in these communities, we grow up immersed in this cycle. With nearly all of our male relatives able to pass on only knowledge from the streets regarding how to survive economically, we are roped into the same outcome. We genuinely don't know anything different, and limited knowledge of life outside the streets nurtures a mentality and disposition that in many ways doesn't prepare us for a successful life outside our environment. We do criminal activity before we actually think about the long-term impacts of our choices. But while the youth in communities like South Side are raised under drastically different circumstances than those in middle- and upper-class communities, we are held to the same standards. Legally and socially, we are expected to have solutions to these complex and overwhelming problems—in other words, we are expected to live by a standard that essentially tells us, "You are responsible for knowing better than to live the way you were raised."

The vast majority of residents in these low-income and high-unemployment communities are not involved in crime and pay taxes so the police can protect them from those who are. Even the wealthiest communities have a segment of people who choose to live an illegal and rebellious lifestyle. The difference is that the wealth, tax revenue, and political representation of those communities keep everyone relatively safe. In impoverished communities, the gangs, hustlers, dope dealers, and pimps are able to take over because the sociopolitical and economic landscape in underserved areas doesn't offer protection for poor men and women.

As inadvertent as it may be, protection and stability in disadvantaged communities rests almost solely in the hands of the residents. Communities like those found in South Side have such a lack of socioeconomic strength that they have to rely on the criminals to do right, which rarely ever happens.

THE SUPPRESSION EQUATION

By the end of the Vietnam War in 1975, the problems in inner-city Chicago could no longer be seen as circumstantial poverty. Veterans returning there from a war they didn't understand in the first place now felt they were prisoners in a domestic war zone—a zone where opportunities were strangled by discriminatory laws, practices, and social attitudes.

For example, women with children who had enrolled in government assistance programs were not permitted to have a man in the home under the programs' requirements, which were enforced through regular home checks. As a result, many men began staying elsewhere until they could gain employment, but employment opportunities became fewer and farther between as businesses and industries moved out. Manufacturing jobs and other skilled labor opportunities decreased, with the overall labor demand shrinking as industries advanced technologies, tapped into international labor forces, or simply downsized their operations due to a reduced demand for their domestic products and services. All of these economic variables impacted the entire country, but when there's a drought, the driest areas typically experience the most devastating effects.

Imagine yourself in this complicated set of circumstances:

You are part of an entire generation returning from war, only to find that the civil injustice and inequality you left behind is still there and waiting for you upon your return. In practice, you are still not treated as equal in the face of the law, government, or general public of your own country. Many of the prominent figures advocating on your behalf have been killed, and you discover that the most applicable jobs with wages capable of supporting a family are virtually nonexistent in your community, whose social and physical borders have been forged over centuries of racial segregation.

Your family has turned to government assistance to help compensate, but as a man, if you reside in the household they will no longer qualify for such programs. You decide to find a way to be with your children without being in the household. There are others in the community facing the same dilemma, so you negotiate other living situations to stay close by your family, but now you're putting the family relationships and dynamics at risk by living with someone else and not being well positioned for contributing financially. The strain on your relationships becomes too great, and you inevitably abandon your family entirely.

These new dilemmas come with their own set of challenges. If you abandon your children due to this stress, you will owe money for child support because you can't live at home. But your job opportunities are limited, so how do you come up with the money? If you don't pay child support, you're going to go to jail. If you don't find a way to make money legally, you're going to go to jail. Your options are razor thin, and your frustration expands daily.

To make matters worse, war and the increasingly violent environment of your community has trauma-tized you to the point that you find yourself struggling to live a functional life, much less find the strength to overcome the adversities before you to integrate into a society largely bent on keeping you where you are. You have to find a way to make money, despite not being ready or equipped for the job market. You look around and ask yourself what's available in your community to provide a livable wage for yourself and your family. And what you see is that a huge crack cocaine and heroin industry has exploded in the community, on the backs of addicted veter-ans with pensions and a community ravaged with trauma and despair.

For you, and for many other returning veterans of the Vietnam War, the profit from illegal drug sales comes easily and frequently, and it is an easy market to get into. To get a job selling drugs, you don't need a resume, connections outside of your community, or prior work experience. With a little training and mentorship, you are molded, affiliated, and indoctrinated into the underground drug trade, and you immediately start making hundreds, if not thousands, of dollars a week selling heroin and crack cocaine to scores of addicts, with new and repeat "customers" perpetuating the demand every day. Given your situation and desperation, it would be almost impossible to say no to several thousand dollars a month to ensure your family's survival and financial security.

As illustrated in this scenario, the duress of the inner city had found in the drug trade both a new economy and a crippling painkiller, but there was a new war gaining traction to combat even the most desperate recourse.

THE WAR ON DRUGS

From the 1980s through the 1990s, the Reagan, Bush, and Clinton administrations expanded funding for policies that had their genesis in Nixon's militarized "War on Drugs" initiative, which aimed to curb the swelling drug epidemic that was sweeping across inner cities throughout the country.

The mystery was, and still is, exactly how and why the epidemic came to be in the first place.

One explanation was offered in the scandalous "Dark Alliance" newspaper series from *San Jose Mercury* journalist Gary Webb, who investigated a disturbing connection between the CIA, inner-city drug dealers, and the Contras, a confederation of rebel groups funded by the United States to oppose Nicaragua's socialist regime in the mid-1990s. Webb followed an import-export trail of cocaine and cash from the streets of South Central Los Angeles to a ring of ousted Nicaraguan politicians, and ultimately to the doorstep of Contra-affiliated drug cartels operating with, as he alleged, CIA approval and support. Webb was eventually disgraced and exiled from mainstream journalism after key sources from the series either disappeared or changed their story. Major newspapers pounced on the predicament by questioning the evidence of his claims, which Webb argued was an attack launched by renowned journalists and publications to save face for not breaking the exposé of the decade themselves. He defended his reporting for years and turned to the emerging Internet of the late 1990s to continue writing on the crack-cocaine conspiracy, racial profiling in police corruption cases, and other unpopular topics. Before his death, Webb wrote about his "Dark Alliance" series in Hugh Wilford's book, *The Mighty Wurlitzer: How the CIA Played America:* "The reason I'd enjoyed such smooth sailing for so long hadn't been, as I'd assumed, because I was careful and diligent and good at my job. The truth was that, in all those years, I hadn't written anything important enough to suppress. . . ." Webb was found with two bullet wounds to the head inside his home in 2004, a shooting that was later ruled a suicide by the Sacramento County coroner.

If Webb was correct, the heightened trafficking of cocaine during the 1980s, which acted as fuel to the fire already burning in the inner cities and beyond, was partially the US government's doing. The absurdity thickens when considering how state, federal, and county governments have subsequently spent trillions in tax revenue to arrest, investigate, and imprison drug offenders, most commonly those dealing or using crack cocaine.

By the end of the 1980s, the number of arrests for drug offenses rose by more than 120 percent.[1] The Federal Bureau of Prisons would later report that by the close of 1999, more than 57 percent of the federal prison population had been sentenced for a drug offense.[2]

Strict policies that failed to address the deeper issues behind the problems resulted in the already struggling black inner-city communities being hit the hardest. Sentencing for crack in particular jumped to outrageous proportions under legislation like the Anti-Drug Abuse Act of 1986, which helped enforce a one hundred to one disparity between sentences for crack cocaine and powder cocaine. This equated to an offender possessing five grams of crack being

---

1 J Austin and A D McVey, "NCCD Prison Population Forecast, 1989: The Impact of the War on Drugs," Abstract, *National Criminal Justice Reference Service*, 1989, https://www.ncjrs.gov/App/Publications/abstract.aspx?ID=122794.
2 U.S. Department of Justice, *Compendium of Federal Justice Statistics*, 1999, NCJ186179, April 2001.

sentenced to a minimum of five years in prison, compared to an offender with five hundred grams of powdered cocaine receiving the same sentence. Because crack was, and is, much less expensive than powdered cocaine, it was most likely to be found in poorer communities. As the 1990s drew to a close, prison population reports from the Bureau of Justice Statistics revealed that black Americans accounted for more than 45 percent of all state and federal prisoners,[3] more than 36 percent of all state prisoners convicted of drug offenses, and 42 percent of all drug-related parole violations,[4] despite representing less than 15 percent of the national population. When the smoke cleared, roughly 9 percent of all black males in their early twenties had been incarcerated.[5]

Some of this had to do with a high number of black men selling crack and other drugs to compensate for their lack of job opportunities. Relatively high rates of usage for high-offense drugs, such as heroin and crack cocaine, and a heavy law-enforcement presence in black communities with the primary purpose of making arrests also contributed to the disproportionate imprisoning of black Americans.

A Bureau of Justice Statistics report from 1995 examined the racial disparities in drug arrests and sentencing to answer the growing concerns of the time. The department's senior statistician, Patrick A. Langan, followed three factors for determining the risk of arrest and length of sentences for

---

3 Allen J. Beck, Ph.D., "Prisoners in 1999," *Bureau of Justice Statistics Bulletin*, August 2000, NCJ183476, http://www.bjs.gov/content/pub/pdf/p99.pdf.
4 E. Ann Carson and Daniela Golinelli, "Prisoners in 2011: Trends in Admissions and Releases, 1991-2012," *Bureau of Justice Statistics Bulletin*, December 2014, NCJ243920, http://www.bjs.gov/content/pub/pdf/p12tar9112.pdf.
5 Allen J. Beck, Ph.D., "Prisoners in 1999."

offenders: type of drug used, frequency of use, and place of use. Referencing data from a survey conducted by the Department of Health and Human Service's Substance Abuse and Mental Health Services Administration that same year, the report found that of all black drug users who reported using illicit drugs, 20 percent said the drug was heroin or cocaine, the type with the greatest risk of arrest. In contrast, according to the report, 16 percent of white drug users reported using heroin or cocaine. There were differences in frequency as well, with the survey finding that "among black drug users, 54 percent reported using drugs at least monthly and 32 percent reported using them weekly. Such frequent drug use was less common among white drug users. Among white users, 39 percent reported using drugs monthly and 20 percent reported using them weekly."

But most revealing to the nucleus of the problem was the report's findings on place of use. "Large metropolitan areas are where 44 percent of Americans live and where 47 percent of illicit drug use occurs but where 60 percent of drug possession arrests occur. With respect to place of residence, the races differ in ways that place black drug users at greater risk of arrest than white users. Large metropolitan areas are where 60 percent of blacks live but where 41 percent of whites live. Moreover, large metropolitan areas are where 63 percent of black drug use occurs compared to 45 percent of white drug use."[6]

---

6 Patrick A. Langan, Ph.D., "The Racial Disparity in U.S. Drug Arrests," National 7 Criminal Justice Reference Services, October 1995, NCJ174600, http://www.bjs.gov/content/pub/pdf/rdusda.pdf.

Adhering to the trifecta of statistical arrest risk—drug type, frequency, and place of use—Langan determined that black drug users should account for 23 percent of possession arrests, but he drew a blank when explaining why that number was actually 36 percent. "The analysis leaves unexplained 13 percentage points," he admitted. "Perhaps the 13 percentage points or some portion of them reflect a practice of police unjustifiably over-arresting blacks, but not necessarily." The report did not examine why black drug sellers, representing 16 percent of all admitted drug sellers, comprised 49 percent of arrests for selling drugs between 1991 and 1993.

But on the streets, all these numbers hinted at more than what political statisticians hypothesizing the problem could see. People were turning to drugs, both as a self-prescribed therapy and a viable commodity, to cope with the hopelessness spun from generations of unresolved traumas and limited opportunities. Desperation gradually led to disproportionate crime statistics, which influenced negative racial stereotypes among segments of society and, in effect, segments of current law enforcement personnel and practices. Over the next several years, a new set of statistics emerged: one in three black males would be imprisoned during his lifetime.

As street leaders with major influence on the youth were arrested, inner-city communities lost their most effective means for affecting change with at-risk youth. The youth who served under these gang leaders didn't know what to do, so they reverted to what they had been taught—the same lifestyle that we're still trying to get kids away from.

While taking major gang leaders off the street seemed like the right thing, it created a ripple effect of explosive violence and division as their followers fought for power, prompting scared residents, many of whom were already distrustful of law enforcement, to withdraw any and all police cooperation.

In the case of black communities, their conditions were such that nearly all chances for black men to succeed were squeezed out, little by little, while at the same time the prison industrial complex began, today accounting for nearly a quarter of the world's prison population[7] and the 90 percent increase of prisoners held in private prisons since 1999.[8]

Lurking in the seldom-discussed shadows was the 200 percent increase in total number of private prisons between 1990 and 2000, with just two of the estimated twenty private prison companies, Corrections Corporation of America (CCA) and the GEO Group, slurping up roughly $2.9 billion annually in state and federal funds to alleviate overcrowded public facilities.[9] As author and journalist Matt Taibbi pointed out in his 2014 book *The Divide: American Injustice in the Age of the Wealth Gap*, major companies invested in the business of imprisonment, which helped to raise the stock value of CCA from $8 a share in 1990 to $30 a share in 2000.

---

7 "Highest to Lowest - Prison Population Total," World Prison Brief, http://www. prisonstudies.org/highest-to-lowest/prison-population-total?field_region_taxonomy_ tid=All.

8 "Prisoners in 2014," Bureau of Justice Statistics, September 2015, NCJ248955, http://www.bjs.gov/content/pub/pdf/p14_Summary.pdf.

9 "Gaming the System: How the Political Strategies of Private Prison Companies Promote Ineffective Incarceration Policies," Justice Policy Institute, June 2011, http:// www.justicepolicy. org/uploads/justicepolicy/documents/gaming_the_system.pdf.

After belly-flopping a meteoric drug policy into the shallowest pools of American society, the highest number of incarcerated individuals in national history rippled with dollar signs. The for-profit prison industry had become one of the safest investments around, placing its bets directly against the people it was now charged with rehabilitating.

FAMILY DYNAMICS

For my siblings and me, the drug epidemic and stern policies to punish it came crashing into our home rather literally. We were pushed into the system after my father's own arrest on the North Side of Chicago. He was charged with the intent to sell and sentenced to nine months in prison, and since my mother lost her custody rights, we were taken into social service custody after he was booked. All of this I learned in pieces throughout my childhood, but it wasn't until I had conversations with my family several years later that I learned the whole story about my parents' lifestyle at the time.

"Why couldn't my mother get custody?" This story took me back to June of 1991, when my brother Cedric, then in his early twenties, walked into my mother's house and found a disturbing sight—my younger brother Aaron, just nine months old at the time, laying beside my mother as she sat in the bed smoking crack cocaine. My mother was also six months pregnant at the time.

Cedric was upset and yelled at her. "What the fuck you doing?! Why you smoking that shit in front of them kids? What's wrong with you?"

My mom became irate and began cursing at him, telling him to mind his business and get out. Their altercation turned aggressive, ending with Cedric's arrest and time in the state penitentiary.

Three months later, my younger sister Samantha was born. Not long before her birth, Chicago had enacted several laws to protect children born to women abusing hard drugs, stating that a woman found with illegal substances in her body at the time of pregnancy was accountable to the Department of Children and Family Services. When Samantha was born, she was found with cocaine in her system, and my mom was summoned to trial.

When she was first visited by the Department of Children and Family Services in 1991, she was informed of her legal rights and questioned about her substance abuse. From the beginning, social workers told her in honest and frank terms, "You have no idea what you're up against. These people will take your kids, lock your ass up, and forget all about you. They don't care about your kids. Whatever drugs your doing, you need to stop it now. And get rid of that attitude because these people will use anything and everything against you." Her first reaction was to say, "Stay out of my business. I'm a good mother to my children." She was ordered to appear at a series of court hearings to determine whether she should retain custody.

My mother, anguished and terrified over the threat of losing her children, frequently lashed out during those hearings. Nearly everything in her life had been controlled in some way by a system of government that had failed to adequately support the people it was supposedly serving, proving again and again to my mother a lack of commitment toward understanding her trauma or any sympathy for her mental and emotional condition. Her emotional outbursts damaged the perception of her character, helping to paint an image of someone unfit for parenting. She was sentenced to anger management and rehab classes, both of which she struggled to complete.

Ultimately, her unstable emotions and lack of self-control and cooperation in court proceedings forced the system's hand, and by the summer of 1993, my mother had permanently lost custody of us. The courts relinquished all custody rights to my father. Approximately a year and a half later my father was arrested, and six of us became wards of the state.

This policy, enacted to protect children from drug abuse and its adverse effects, essentially made a hospital's infant ward the scene of the crime. Drug-addicted parents were summoned to trial immediately after the birth of their child, and, after failed attempts to overcome years of drug use, they were sentenced to lose custody of their children. For mothers in particular, this is a much more devastating sentence than jail itself, as the one thing they want most in their life is their children.

By the time I was born, my parents had been using drugs for an excess of twenty years. Like so many, recovery for my parents seemed virtually impossible. Unfortunately, their inability to overcome their addictions validated everything that politicians, law enforcement, government officials, and the general public already think about people in poor communities, especially people from the housing projects—which is that they evade responsibility. The perception is that they don't want to get themselves together and work hard to be contributing members of society—that they just take advantage of the system instead of focusing on themselves and how they can get better.

When my mother's mother found out about the case, she advised family not to take custody of my mother's children. "Listen. Do not take her kids. All she's going to do is give you her kids so that you can take care of them, and then she's not going to want to get well. She needs to do what she has to do to get her children back. Don't give her a reason to avoid that. Don't bail her out. Let her do this herself. Let her deal with this."

For the longest time, my mother resented my grandmother for that. When my grandmother was diagnosed with cancer in 1995, she called my mom to her deathbed to say some last words to her. Hardened and unforgiving, my mother didn't go, and just a few months later, her mother passed away. Her DCFS caseworker, Mr. Ramsey, relayed the news to her; however, she remained cold and seemingly unshaken by the news, given her traumatic preoccupation with her children being taken away.

She didn't go to the funeral, and she didn't reach out. She was nowhere to be found. At the time, she was not even bothered by what had happened.

She turned against her family, and her family turned against her. Nearly everything that could have gone wrong for my mother—both that year and in those critical years of her youth—did go wrong, and she was never able to recover from her past to better face her future.

It's a common theme within impoverished communities. Like millions of others, my mother's emotions largely drove her actions and inactions, mostly because years of duress had left her more or less unable to control them. She was consumed with anger and frustration. Unfortunately, most don't understand the consequences of their anger until it's too late. For people in poverty, there is very little cushion to save you when you make a mistake.

My mother experienced an enormous amount of traumatic life circumstances—from her childhood abuse, to living through her brother's murder at a young age, to losing her children, to a perpetual and life-altering drug addiction. She rarely felt she had complete control over her life. Her response to the tragic events of her life has always been to get harder and colder, and consequently, the pain never stops. This condition is the essence of deep psychosocial trauma, and it permeates across generations of poor and disenfranchised communities all across the nation.

BLAMING THE VICTIMS

We can never fully understand a perspective outside of our own, but to begin to understand the mind-set and hardened condition of someone like my mother, one has to know the cycle of abuse and neglect they've been through. To add to the trauma that she had never recovered from, her lack of control led to a final blow: having what meant more to her than anything else—her children—taken away. Leaving a person like that out in the world to figure it out on their own is just shy of insanity. We can't expect people to navigate their own rehabilitation after going through an entire lifetime's worth of depravity.

Ideally, all survivors of childhood trauma, like my mother, would receive nurturing from a community of like-minded, supportive individuals and be given all the services they need for psychosocial and emotional recovery, such as spiritual counseling, mental health counseling, physical therapy, and group support. Instead of month-to-month checkups from a social worker, they would be evaluated for several months on an intensive, day-to-day basis to ensure they were getting everything they needed to begin recovering from generations of poverty and social failure.

This type of holistic support takes an abundance of money, resources, trauma care, and policy changes. However, with a limited government budget and no political representation from poor communities of color, it is unlikely that we will acquire this support from government assistance alone.

On the other hand, we have an opportunity to be more strategic in how we use the resources we do have, such as counseling, therapy, rehabilitation, and making sure the recovery is successful so that the impoverished can enter society as working, fully rehabilitated citizens who can perform the duties of parents and contributing members of society. However, with systemic racism and oppression still woven into the economic and political fabric of our social order, we will continue to see one tragedy after another.

Everything about how our society, government, and marketplace have responded to the struggles of poor communities of color—by capitalizing on the social failures while ignoring the economic and political structures that create them—forms a striking image of how systemic discrimination, even after legal change, becomes oppression through neglect, whether it be due to race, class, or both. The narrow-viewed drug laws and law-enforcement strategies targeting inner cities, the disproportionate increase of black inmates and their length of sentences, the profits from an imprisoned workforce, the growing disenfranchisement of the poor, the increase of private investments in prisons as a business—it all coalesces into an image of societal indifference, political negligence, institutional corruption, and a great deal of inhumanity for those left to find a way out of a hellish world most pretend doesn't exist.

My story is rare. Rising from such beginnings to an Ivy League education occurred with a lot of hard work and help from others. But for the majority who don't get the help or have the same strength of determination, they will never get a quality education, which means they will likely never get a well-paying job or a position of power capable of facilitating real change.

In the case of professionals and politicians and their affiliation with poor communities, information without a personal relationship or connection to the community can be just as dangerous as ignorance itself. Educators, sociologists, psychologists, economists, and others have studied these issues backward and forward, brainstorming ways to mitigate and assist parents who are experiencing catastrophic life struggles, like being incarcerated for criminal activity or abusing drugs, so that they can recover and be fit parents again. These were esteemed analysts and educators working on solutions to the problems, but the one critical element missing was a personal relationship and engagement with the communities. Even if we presume policy makers genuinely had the best interests of poor communities at heart, they used their outside analytics to assess the conditions of those communities without understanding the more critical elements, such as key historic events in the community, the family dynamics, social and political perspectives, and their respective traumas. You cannot truly protect and serve a community that you do not know, love, and understand. Social theory and political equations can never calculate the lived experience. The one thing most policy makers never did was go into the community and work to truly understand what the people were experiencing inside their homes and on the streets.

If you don't ask the people you're impacting what would help them—what improvements could be made to benefit all parties involved—then we're not truly respecting their intelligence or their struggle. Instead, some policy makers assumed they could solve the problem on the community's behalf. They went to the board, wrote down half-cooked game plans, and executed a series of trial-and-error ideas that ultimately reaped unintended consequences in the community.

For the youth who experience the prison complex at an early age, true rehabilitation means that they never go back. But the majority of people who go into prison, especially for low-level drug offenses, go right back in. They are not taught to do anything different from what got them there in the first place, nor are they given the critical help necessary to do something different. That negative affirmation becomes their reality.

A similar situation is occurring within our inner cities. Some gang factions are making an excess of $1,000,000 a year in the drug trade, and the policies created to ignite the War on Drugs have actually perpetuated the proliferation of drugs in the country. To bring about real change, we have to change the narrative. Given that the drug trade is so successful, in part because of the supply and demand, we have to focus more on public health and safety, legislation that will eliminate the economic viability of the drug trade, and initiatives that will aid the process of recovery and rehabilitation for drug addicts.

On the subject of depravity, when the people of a community are starving to have basic needs met, they will find a way to survive under those circumstances. For most poor and neglected communities, the drug trade is the only viable market suitable for the residents to earn a living and adequately support themselves. Some residents feel that they have no choice under their circumstances, and telling a struggling community it can't have things because of the methods it was forced to use to get them creates a lose-lose situation. Communities will do whatever they feel they have to do because they need what everyone else needs, but in the end, that desperation for survival is criminalized, and the cycle starts all over again.

Penal systems and correctional institutions certainly have their place in society, but reprimanding in the absence of sufficient rehabilitative and reintegration initiatives is destructive. If our system reprimands someone but doesn't teach them how to make themselves stronger, smarter, and capable of improving their life, then the problems within our communities shouldn't be too puzzling. Our current strategy is a recipe for disaster, where a cycle of crime and violence is the only outcome.

On the subject of policing, our communities value policing that protects against crimes like murder, rape, assault, robbery, and so on, but once trust is lost we lose the most essential element in the relationship between the people who must enforce the laws and the people who have to abide by them. If that trust is gone, we have to work hard to earn it back. However, time has shown that on a macro level, poor communities have not substantially seen changes in policies that reflect the system's genuine effort to rebuild that trust and confidence, as communities are still struggling with poverty, education, violence, mental health, and hopelessness.

From an economic perspective, those who make the most money pay the most taxes to live in the best places. This is why wealth is so intrinsically connected to safety, well-being, and success. The more money you have, the better your ability to move into a neighborhood that's safe. The less money you have, the more likely you'll end up in an area of poverty that's dangerous and violent, as the resources aren't made available to keep the community safe. Poverty and violence are not synonymous with each other, but if you don't have the resources or power of influence to create lasting, positive change, then the criminal element will move in and establish strong ties within the social order.

Given that poverty and crime coincide in such plain view, we can also see a glaring disparity in the relationship between criminal activity and economic stability, when there really should be none. But this is the unfortunate reality for poor people. If given $100,000, most poor youth living in dangerous and deprived neighborhoods would tell you, "I'm going to buy a big house for my mom. I'm going to buy a big house for my family so we can all live there." They wouldn't buy a big house in their current community. They would purchase their home on another side of town—the North Side, in Chicago's case—or the suburbs, where more land is available and affordable.

However, it's about more than money and wealth. It's also about the idea of living in a safe environment so that you don't have to worry about walking down the street every day. In an ideal world, you could give a person $100,000 and they wouldn't have the inclination to leave their community but instead would want to invest in it. And in no world should children be afraid to walk to school for fear of being shot or spend their childhood forcibly separated from their family.

CHAPTER FOUR

NO EASY WAY OUT

I was seventeen when I finally moved back in with my parents. But as I was settling into the life I had spent so many years fighting for, I got a reality check. I had been so focused on getting home that when I actually got there I was faced with hard realities about their drug use and lifestyle that I had not expected. All I ever wanted was to live with my parents again, but I had romanticized the goal without considering the day-to-day struggles my parents were going through.

The summer I moved home was a great time in my life. I was the happiest I had ever been. My parents and I were elated to be reunited with one another, and we spent a lot of time talking about the past and enjoying the day-to-day experience of being together. Things as simple as laying on the couch watching TV, cooking ramen noodles and hotdogs in the microwave, or my mom frying chicken and all of us sitting on the couch eating together brought me real joy. I feel like when I was in foster care, I had happy moments but never joy. Spending time with my real family, in my mind, was the true essence of joy.

Long before I moved back in with them, however, their marriage had become tumultuous. Daily arguments and petty disagreements had become the norm. My mom would habitually tell me that I'd never really met my dad. She would say, "The man you see in front of you now is not your real father. Your real father hasn't been around for a while. I'm not even sure you ever met your father—the sober one, the one before he started using drugs and acting crazy."

She would tell me that at one point in their life together they'd had a good relationship, contrary to what I usually saw with them. Over time, as the romance faded and complacency set in, negative personality traits and habits got in the way of their lifestyle and relationship.

For the majority of my life, I remember my father taking the brunt of my mother's anger and frustration, whether it was because of him or something else. However, whenever my mother would reflect, she would tell me he was a good man when they first met. She spoke of how handsome he was and how he used to dress really nice. He was a true gentleman, and they had a deep affection for one another. They treated each other with respect and really enjoyed being around one another, staying up late into the night talking about anything and everything. But as time went on, things changed.

Drugs, for the most part, made them do things they weren't accustomed to doing, and their habit just took over the relationship. Over time, their marriage became less about adoration and affection and more about financial dependency and obligation.

Now, at any given moment at home, conversation between them would end in cursing and screaming. "Back in the day, your dad used to be decent. He took care of himself. Now it's just gotten worse over the years. He's no good to nobody. And his people warned me about him, too. He's not the man I want you to grow up to be. He's not the man I want any of my kids to grow up to be. He's a poor excuse for a man, let alone a father."

My father's veteran's benefits supported the household. He's 100 percent disabled, so his income, for the most part, paid the bills and supported them financially every month. Aside from the money they spent to pay their bills, nearly everything left over was going toward buying and using drugs or paying others back. That's really what their lifestyle had been throughout most of their marriage, and they didn't take the initiative to live beyond that. For my parents, and many other residents in the Englewood community, what started off as recreational drug use turned into a necessity—a chemical dependency.

I was starting to realize that my parents' financial obligation to one another had orchestrated their relationship over the years and formed the basis for their dependency on one another. They were constantly at odds with one another, but for many years they always came together to use drugs. They went to the same places and knew the same people. They both had associations with the people who sold to them. They were in communities of like-minded people who had all developed drug habits. In effect, they built their entire lives around drugs, so to remove that element would have meant rebuilding everything they knew.

CONFLICT OF WILL

Less than three weeks after moving back in with my parents, my first goal was to find a job. My junior year of high school was nearing an end, and I wanted to head into the summer with some way to keep myself busy when I wasn't at home. I sent applications out all over Chicago and was accepted as an intern at the Chicago Summer Business Institute, which took juniors and seniors in high school to intern at different corporations around the city. Through this internship, I began working at two places. One was the food services company Aramark and the other was Starbucks, both of which were located in the Chase Tower in downtown Chicago.

I was working in the basement cafeteria, where all the employees of the Chase Tower went to purchase food.

I was responsible for cleaning the countertops and glasses, sweeping the floors, and stocking napkins and utensils. As my first employment opportunity, and it being in downtown Chicago, I felt excited to have the opportunity.

I got paid every two weeks, my first experience of getting money for myself. While it felt good to be paid, it wasn't too long after I joined the program that issues with my parents and money came up.

Every now and again, I would go home and they would ask me for $10, $15, or $20 whenever they needed it. In the beginning, it didn't bother me. I never really understood my parents' lifestyle, so I didn't think much of it and didn't mind being able to help. I never really knew what they were doing with the money, and I didn't really care to know. I knew they'd had trouble with drugs in the past, and I knew that even though they were parents, they still had a life, so I didn't question it. I was naive to both the psychological and physiological toll of the drug epidemic in my community. My parents, having done such a great job hiding their drug use from us, knew I was ignorant of their condition and, at times, used that to their advantage.

These issues became aggravating when my parents would ask for money and not pay me back. They also tended to ask for money days before they were paid at the beginning of the month. I was only making internship money, and after lending to my parents, I would sometimes end up broke at the end of my pay period. That caused the beginnings of friction.

That summer was an introduction to the reality of their lifestyle and seeing firsthand why they had never been able to raise us normally. I started my last year of school frustrated and a little confused. Throughout my earlier life, I had never been asked what I wanted to be when I grew up, and even if I had been asked, I probably would have just said I wanted to go home. All my energy over those thirteen years in foster care had gone toward getting back home. It took so much emotional energy, in fact, that I'd never had enough energy left over to think about anything else. Now that I was home, I really had no direction at all. My limbo worsened during my last year of high school because I felt like I had spent all my energy and time fighting for a lost cause—for people who didn't have the strength or even the will to get themselves right. And as a result I had missed out trying to figure out what I wanted to do with my life in the long term.

I tried to talk to my parents about their problems and got two very different reactions. In the beginning, my mom didn't handle those conversations very well. She'd get upset that I was talking to her about her drug abuse, and she'd be quick to blame my father for their drug problems. When I said I was losing money to help support their habits, she'd get upset every time and become very emotional and defensive.

When I talked to my dad about it, he always lied about what he did and made me feel wrong for feeling the way I was feeling. For many reasons, I was much harsher on my dad when it came to his drug use. Aside from the fact that he perpetually lied to me, I felt that his role as the man meant a lot more in the family dynamic. I wanted him to truly feel how this impacted his family. My father does not get defensive or confrontational, so the anger I couldn't express to my mother I took out on my dad.

Talks with both of them, however, never went anywhere. After a few months, I started looking for other places to stay, sometimes spending nights at our neighbor's apartment upstairs and other times staying with high school friends for days and weeks. I would always let my parents know when I was leaving to be with friends, and they never questioned my whereabouts. Whenever I left for extended periods of time, I made sure to check in with them and let them know that I was all right and that I wasn't far away. I was eighteen years old, and I was at the beginning of transitioning out of their home, but I'm not sure if they knew that or thought to question it.

When you have a strong family foundation, a lot of money, community support, and opportunity, you can afford to be in limbo. When you put your mind to something and have the resources available to do it, you can usually achieve your goal relatively easily. If you're a student who's been nurtured in a relatively stable household by two parents, who can afford to put your education and social well-being first, then that foundation is a great platform to build on. But I realized that I would never get that foundation from my parents, and that was very difficult to accept.

By the time I was in this limbo, I didn't have the grades I thought I needed to go to a good school, and I felt that was because I hadn't put enough effort into my education. I didn't have money to invest in any business idea or project that I wanted to do to make myself accessible. I didn't have parents who could give me mentorship or guidance toward a successful future. They never pushed college on me, and they couldn't teach me the ins and outs of building a successful life, because they had never done anything to be successful themselves. The best way I learn is by example, so I was at a severe disadvantage in that regard.

The example that my parents set didn't motivate or inspire me. I had no real outlet or guidance to help nurture my quest for opportunities, and that really frustrated me. Living in a community filled with drugs, alcoholism, and homelessness didn't provide me with any resources to do what I wanted to do with my life. But seeing the reality of what I'd spent so long fantasizing about forced me to make hard choices that I may have been too comfortable to make otherwise. My environment at home pushed me to create truer, stronger visions of who I was and who I wanted to be. If I was going to find a way out, I knew that I wouldn't be finding it at home. I would have to determine my fate on my own terms, for better or for worse.

CHAPTER
FIVE

SECOND CHANCES

My relationship with my high school dean began during a day in detention. It was the fall semester of my senior year at ACE Tech, and between the turmoil at home and my internships around Chicago, my class participation was almost nonexistent. I remember I hadn't slept the night before, so I skipped class, which landed me in the office for a detention slip.

When I arrived after school, several other students were waiting outside classroom 209—the detention room. The assistant dean, Mr. Contreras, walked up to us and made us stand in a line. "Don't say a word," he said. "All you guys know why you're here. You stand here in a straight line. I don't know what you all thought you were going to do after school, but right now you belong to me. You're on my time. So stand here and don't say a word."

Then the dean came out and escorted us into the detention room. He told us to sit down and be quiet. He introduced himself as Mr. McGrone. After surveying the room and getting everyone in order, he turned his attention to me. Later, he told me there was something about me that sparked his interest, something in that moment that stood out. After detention, he asked me to stay behind to learn what my story was.

When I was in school, I never had behavioral problems. I was not a bad kid. I never got an attitude. I never fought anybody. I never gave teachers a hard time with my attitude or anything like that. I was sent to detention a few times for minor things, like skipping class, falling asleep in class, or not doing homework, but I was never a problem student. I just wasn't motivated to be there and struggled to make school a priority in my life.

While we were in detention, many students seemed to have behavioral problems. I was one of the only ones sitting there quiet and obedient. I was distraught and stressed, and I felt the gravity of life weighing down on me all the time—and to my dean, that came off as humility. He really valued humility, as it usually manifests in someone who has experienced deep struggles and trauma. He looked at me and could tell I was going through a lot and that my actions in detention weren't the result of a class clown or problem child.

Days later, he followed up with me to have a one-on-one conversation about what was going on in my life. I didn't trust him at first, so I didn't tell him more than just briefly about my time in foster care. He seemed genuinely interested in my story, pushing gently for more details without making me uncomfortable. I told him that I had just gotten out of a bad situation with a foster parent and that I was living at home with my parents. I explained to him how they made me angry all the time because they were borrowing what little money I earned and not paying it back. I told him that I felt compelled to give it to them because I was living in their house but that it didn't seem entirely fair because they were getting so much money at the beginning of the month.

"They spend it all," I told him. "I don't know where that money goes. I just hate that they get so much money and they're always asking me for money. It's really putting a strain on our relationship."

I told him that I was frustrated because it's very hard to say no to my parents. "When they ask me for money like this, it really makes me upset. It bothers me that I can't have a good relationship with my parents without them always asking me for money."

I confessed that most days, I just stayed at school all day to stay away from home, which is what I'd decided I had to do in order to accept their lives and financial problems. I wasn't motivated to do anything in school, which he took at face value, and we left it at that.

A ROPE APPEARED

"I have orientation for this program that I'm starting up. I want you to come to it," Mr. McGrone told me the day after my detention.

I had no idea what to expect, and I was confused as to why he cared so much about us, but I was intrigued to find out. I didn't really want to go home after school anyway, so I decided to go . . . along with about half of the senior class.

It was immediately following the last class of the day in the afternoon, around 3:30, when we met in the gymnasium. He began talking to us in a way that no other teacher or counselor had ever done before. "I'm glad you all are here," he said. "Let me thank you all." Those few words alone were enough to get most of our attention. "You don't have to be here," he continued. "Of all the places you have to be, you could be anywhere, but I'm very honored and thankful that you're here. I want to talk to you about how great I think you all are. This is the first senior class, which means that you all will forever be the original leaders of this school. I want nothing more than to help you guys do the best at whatever it is you want to be."

Then he started talking to us about real-life circumstances that really resonated with all of us. "I come from Gary, Indiana, raised in a family of seventeen brothers and sisters. My community was ravaged with guns and violence. My mother suffered from a mental illness that none of us understood at the time. I had a gun put to my head when I was eighteen, the trigger was pulled, but the gun didn't go off. I graduated high school with a 1.2 GPA. Through the grace of God, I had the right people come into my life and set me on the right path. I graduated from college with a 3.65. Here I am, standing here today, the dean of this school. Many of you are going through things. I know there are a lot of you in this room going through things that most people wouldn't imagine you are going through."

He said, "Someone in here has a father who left them. They really hate that their father isn't around anymore. They're really angry about it. Someone just lost a mother. Someone's cousin was just shot down on the street last weekend. That really got them messed up. They don't understand why they lost their cousin like that. Someone's mother and father are struggling with drug abuse. They're never home. They always create struggle. They always fight. Someone's parents just got a divorce."

He was bringing up real problems that no one bothered to talk about. Because no one ever talked about our trauma, we had just accepted it all as normal circumstances. But by engaging with us in that way, the dean revealed his passion to ignite us, to wake us up. He spoke in such a way that we were compelled to listen. He had a charisma about him and an experience that really drew young people in to listen to what he had to say. He said, "I don't care what you're going through. Remember this: *Life is a fight for territory. Once you stop fighting for what you want, what you don't want will automatically take over.* So keep struggling, soldiers, because your struggles will prepare you for greatness."

Coupled with the fact that he was a strong, willful male, it was obvious he had a gift for helping young people. That rubbed off on many of us that day, and by the end of the meeting, we had all joined his leadership program.

This rite-of-passage initiative, called the Ambassadors program, consisted of sessions every day after school, usually from 3:30 in the afternoon until 6:30 or 7:00 in the evening. We would talk about anything and everything that really served as impediments in our life experiences. Mr. McGrone never talked about class, never asked anybody why they were messing up in class, and never asked anybody what he could do to help them with their academics. In fact, he almost didn't say anything about school at all.

Our sessions illuminated our personal life experiences, and through those intimate discussions we came to understand each other. We came to understand what happened in our lives that was so traumatic and why we never got over those things. Mr. McGrone talked to us about how we could reconcile those problems through his class. It was a process, he told us, and every day we talked about how to handle different situations in our lives. For instance, if someone came in and their mom was struggling with drug abuse, we would talk about addiction and living with addicts for a session. Another day, we would talk about fatherlessness and how it affected us. Different people would talk about how their father left them when they were young and how their father wasn't in the household. Some would talk about how they would watch their fathers beat their mothers. Some would disclose how a family friend molested them when they were younger. We all had our own trauma stories.

The dean helped us open ourselves to a group, which gave us new strength, comfort, and confidence. It gave us a sense of solidarity, and it facilitated bonds of love and trust. During one session we talked about family history, where he instructed us to draw a family tree. He said, "I want you guys to trace back your history. I want you to learn about people in your family who would help you understand why you are the way you are and where you're going." His favorite line was that "if you don't know your history, you're bound to repeat it."

One of the most essential aspects of the leadership program was performing community service and community-oriented activities. Mr. McGrone would have us go around the neighborhood, find homeless people to bring to the school, and host food drives. We would have cookouts on the weekends and have community members come to the school and play basketball. We would have the responsibility of setting up the food and serving the homeless community members when they came to the school.

Community members would come in and line up, and we would serve them a plate of food so they could sit down and eat. While they were eating, Mr. McGrone would make each of us go to a table and eat with a homeless person and get to know them. He would then play music and have the young men dance with the elder ladies. He wrapped up the afternoon by talking about how much our high school loved the community, how we would do anything to help, how we were there for them, and how we really wanted to be involved and engaged. He sought to create that bond with the community.

That really helped the leadership team grow closer, so it became more of a brotherhood and a sisterhood among us. We were like a little fraternity within the school because we all were having these experiences that we hadn't had in our first three years in school.

One day we had to march in the cold. It was December in Chicago, and Mr. McGrone told us to come on a Saturday morning, so no one was excited to be there. We had to wear a black hoodie and blue jeans. He told us to stand in single file. It was all snow and slush on the ground, and I can remember my feet being nearly frozen. He wanted us to march all around the neighborhood. We marched about a mile in the cold and the snow, saying that we loved our community and ACE Tech. He said, "I don't want you to stop. I don't care if you get frostbite. Don't stop until I tell you to stop."

It felt like pledging for a fraternity. Having these struggles together, talking about our personal issues in front of each other, and having our fellow classmates collaborate to come up with peaceful solutions to problems really brought the group together in a major way.

Mr. McGrone was very skilled at finding ways to bring us together. One of the things he did was use one person's story to get to the rest of the group. If you imagine a classroom of fifteen or twenty students all coming from the same type of neighborhood and similar circumstances—growing up with a single mother struggling with poverty, dealing with parents who were drug addicts or alcoholics, living with an unsupportive family in an unsupportive community, constantly being told they were worthless—then you can imagine that the morale was low and the level of distrust high.

One day we were waiting for the session to start, and I was growing impatient because I wanted to be in the session for the first fifteen to twenty minutes before I had to go to basketball practice. On this day, Mr. McGrone came in very upset because he had heard that someone from the leadership team was involved in an altercation earlier in the day. The first thing he said when he came into the room was, "One of our leaders got in trouble today. I give y'all a little bit of power, and this is how you act? This is what I'm doing this for? This is what y'all think about this?"

When no one said anything, he looked around the room and said, "Y'all think y'all bad now? Have y'all forgotten what this process is about?"

Everyone stayed quiet while he scanned our faces. "Responsibility to the school and this community, to serve as an example of what real leadership looks like . . . that's what this is about. When y'all get in trouble for foolishness, you can't be the leaders that this school expects you to be."

As time went on I got really anxious because my coach didn't like us showing up late to basketball practice. As Mr. McGrone was speaking, I went to the back of the room and was trying to go out the door, but before I got out he said, "Where are you going?"

"Well, I've got to go to basketball practice," I said.

"Oh, basketball practice is more important than your life?"

"No, but I already promised my coach that I would go to basketball practice, so I've got to leave."

"Naw, close that door and come back in here," he said with a stern look on his face.

I closed the door and walked back in.

"What the hell are you saying, man? You selfish," he said. "Here you are. You've got all these problems in your life, and you're worrying about damn practice."

I was kind of thrown off. I was taken aback that he was calling me out in front of everyone like that. I felt like I was on the spot, and then he said, "You killing yourself. Here you are. You're damn near homeless. You come to school with the same clothes on. You've slept on benches in the park. Momma and daddy drugged out of their minds. And now you worried about basketball practice? You're not even worried about your own life." I noticed that as he was speaking to me, more students in the class started to get affected by it. Although he was talking to me, he was also talking to the other students through me and my story.

"I can see death in your eyes," he said. "Do you even know why you're here? Why you are even in school? Do you know what you're going to do? Do you know how your parents feel?" He told my whole story in front of all the kids, which embarrassed me at first. Then he said, "You're a coward. You're weak. You just gonna walk out of here and not take this seriously because of some damn game. It's not even going to be here after you leave. You're selfish. You're not doing yourself right."

No one had known that I was in and out of my parents' home until then, and I could see my peers beginning to squirm and some wiping their cheeks as tears streamed down their faces. In one way or another, we were all feeling the same pain. We were all homeless to an extent, and I don't think any of us really believed we knew what it was to be loved selflessly—to have someone truly care about our well-being and nothing else. My story spoke their stories, too, and all at once, we realized how much we had in common. I can't describe the power of that moment.

He was addressing me in a very forceful way and telling me the truth about myself in front of the other students. He was even somewhat humiliating me, but I felt humility more than anger, and it came off as more of a reckoning, a moment of truth among the students.

A lot of my peers got emotional, but a student named Reggie really took it to heart. He had a thing about bullying and truly hated to see other people get bullied. And it looked like my mentor was bullying me, though I had an understanding that this wasn't just about me.

Mr. McGrone said, "I know what you going through, but I don't feel sorry for you at all. I don't pity you. I don't care about none of that stuff. None of that matters. Forget that. Pick yourself back up. I'm not going to cry for you. I don't feel sorry for you. I don't feel sorry for none of you."

Reggie finally stood up, fuming by this point. My mentor said to him, "What's your problem, man?"

"You're the problem," Reggie said.

"What did I do?"

"You know what you're doing. You're out here talking about him and putting his business out there like that. He don't deserve that. You don't know what he's been through. He don't deserve that."

My mentor used that as an opportunity to get to Reggie and his problems. "What do you have against bullying?"

Reggie got quieter and said, "I don't like people to get bullied. I don't like that. It makes me upset, people who pick on other people who are not their size. I don't respect people like that."

Reggie standing up for me took me off guard. I had never really experienced someone supporting me like that before, and strangely enough, having someone else stand up for me made me understand the importance of a story, something worth fighting for. Someone else seeing my value and being willing to fight for me triggered me to see my life in a new way—and what I saw in myself was something worth fighting for. My life was dysfunctional, filled with challenges and sadness, and seeing Reggie's reaction and the reactions of the other students offered some personal validation that my struggle wasn't normal. To my surprise, I was comforted by others hearing about my pain. They showed me that I mattered, despite what I had believed for so long. I realized after that day that Mr. McGrone was using other people's stories to unify us and make us think critically about our life struggles and how we could use each other to overcome them.

His goal was to bring together a leadership team that got over systemic issues so that we could begin to focus on the things that truly mattered in life—forgiving ourselves, reconciling our problems, and focusing on how we were going to succeed together.

The culmination of the program came one day in January 2008. On that day, Mr. McGrone had us doing activities that in my mind were the climax of my experience in the leadership program. I'd had a lot of moments of recovery, rehabilitation, and reconciliation during the program, but there was one moment that transformed the trajectory of my life forever.

Earlier in the program, we'd made paper torches, having no idea what they were for. But as we approached the final week of the program, Mr. McGrone explained himself. "I want you to come to school in white gloves with your torch. I want you to carry your torch everywhere you go. I want you to wear your white gloves everywhere you go. I don't want you to say a word the whole day." We were to do this for an entire week. All of this was part of a test we had to pass—the ultimate challenge before completing the program.

We went the whole day during school without saying a word. We just went to class, carrying our torches with us everywhere we went. At the end of the school day on the last day of the challenge, he said he wanted us to line up single file at the back door of the school. We stood in line for about fifteen to twenty minutes while he went back and forth making sure that everybody was in line and staying quiet and reflective. Mr. McGrone had also asked us to bring a black dress sock to school that day and keep it in our right pocket until he told us to take it out and to bring a brown paper bag, some notebook paper, and a pen.

At 3:35, we were preparing to march out of the school. "No talking," he said. "Just sit there and be quiet." Everyone stayed quiet, and then he marched us across the street to the high school's annex.

There were about thirty of us at the time. Over time, some of the students had decided to quit, deciding they'd had enough of the pledging process. Mr. McGrone had always been okay with that and began telling us halfway through the program, "I know I'm starting off with all you guys, but I don't expect you all to make it. I don't care. All I need is five. I don't care to have all of you finish this program. If I can just get the strongest five, I'm okay with that." But by that time, most of us were too invested in the process to quit. We believed in what we were doing. He wanted to challenge us, to make us feel that if we stuck with it we would really be accomplishing something bigger than ourselves.

As we sat along the wall, he turned off the lights and said, "I want you to take out the paper and pen you have." The lights were turned off, so the room was very dim.

"Now I want you to think about a story, something that happened in your life that was so traumatic that you never told anybody else. I want you to think about something so horrible that you wouldn't dare tell anybody else because it hurt so bad. I want you to write that experience down on a piece of paper in full detail. I want you to forgive yourself for it. You need to know today that it's not your fault. I want you to sit in silence and just write. You don't have to write it appropriately. You don't have to write it correctly. Just write how you feel. I want you to really focus on writing down this event in your life."

Immediately when he gave us the activity, I said, "I've got so much to think about." Then something came to me and I wrote: *I'm sorry. I'm sorry that I failed you.* From that moment on, I never stopped writing. I felt a series of raw emotions come over me, and I started crying and writing at the same time.

Most kids are very reserved when it comes to personal problems. Young black men in particular avoid emotion as much as possible. But because Mr. McGrone made us understand that nobody would ever see it, I felt liberated to write my truth for the first time. In a sense, I felt like I was making peace with myself and God.

I confessed to things I had done that I wasn't proud of, such as lying and stealing, and wrote about how emotionally distressed and tormented I was. I wrote, "I don't know what to make of my life. If there's any way that you can save me from this, please let me know what I have to do. This is a cry out for help." I had never really made a confession like that before, and my heart began to race as my emotions flowed out of me for the first time. I wrote about things I had repressed for so long. I apologized for everything I had done wrong, all the ways I had let myself down. With every event I wrote down, I concentrated on letting go.

My writing got so heavy that I started to rip the paper. I was writing every traumatic event that I had never told anyone, feeling the weight of it all fall from my mind onto the paper. As the session ended, Mr. McGrone came up to me and tapped my shoulder. "I don't want you to stop writing," he said softly. "I want you to write until you finish. I just want you to let it all go."

So I wrote. I wrote page after page until it was all out of me. That moment was what catapulted my life's experience to the other side—the moment that broke the chains that had wrapped around me and confined me to the life I was so determined to transform.

When everyone was finished, he said, "I want everybody in this room . . . everything that you've written on this paper, I want you to rip it up. I want you to rip it up into little pieces. And I want you to put it in this bucket." But he stopped beside my shoulder and told me, "I don't want you to rip yours up. I want you to fold yours four ways and put it in your paper bag." Mr. McGrone had at that moment understood how deep a transformation I was undergoing and knew the significance of keeping the evidence of that transformation.

Everybody else ripped theirs up and put it in the bucket, but I kept mine in the paper bag and put the date on it: January 14, 2008. Then we all went outside. Mr. McGrone put the bucket on the ground and took out some lighter fluid and a lighter. "Before I light this bucket, I want you all to know that this is a reflection of everything that ever happened to you in your life, especially those things that have taken so much energy and life out of you. I want you to know that we are burning all those things on this day. And from this day forward, we are not going to hold on to these things. We are going to let them go. We are going to live our life victoriously and with purpose." Then he had us bow our heads in prayer, and after he prayed, he lit the bucket.

He said, "I want to congratulate all of you. You have just finished the leadership program. Congratulations. You are now part of the ACE Tech Ambassadors program." And with that, the program was over. But my journey with Mr. McGrone was only just beginning.

MENTORING THE
TRAUMATIZED MIND

Rodney stands with Mr. McGrone during a ceremony commemorating
Rodney's completion of the leadership program.

A young person has to experience a moment when they see themselves in a different way. They have to have an encounter so strong that they shift their mind-set. It doesn't have to be a mentor sitting them down in a classroom and telling them to let go. It can literally happen by helping them to envision themselves as adults and seeing where they want their lives to be. One of the most effective ways to inspire and empower young people is through the lens of education and opportunity. We must equip students with the knowledge and the wherewithal to take on the opportunities presented them.

The education that I got from my mentor was a deeper, more profound education than the norm, and it changed the trajectory of my life. It is my belief that young people who are broken are missing this critical form of education in school. More than a trade or a job, they need a deeper level of education, as otherwise they cannot recover from the generations of psychological trauma surging through their community.

This was true in my case because my parents experienced a high level of trauma that really filtered through to their children, who are still experiencing it to this day. By taking me through this emotional and psychological journey to rejuvenate my spirit, my mentor opened my mind to an understanding of the reality of adversity and simultaneously equipped me with the propensity to overcome that adversity. That change in my mentality continues to fuel my success today.

Perhaps this is best explained through the lens of trade. Suppose we experience an engineering boom. Inevitably, firms will open positions for engineers, and kids will go to trade school to learn to be successful engineers. Or, if there's an excess of construction opportunities, kids will train to learn construction, and after eight weeks or so of training, they will be equipped to go into the construction field and be successful.

But there's a different type of education needed for a child living in poverty. We have to strengthen their ability to adapt to any adversity, any challenge, any area of great struggle. If we can teach an individual how to deal with the complexities of life, that's the greatest education we can give, and I have not met anyone other than my mentor, Mr. McGrone, who has done that. Before his leadership program, I had no sense of great ambition and certainly no confidence to pursue my ambitions. But through that program, there really was a shift in my psyche that allowed me to attract success. My other mentors—the mentor who helped me apply for college, get into college, and get scholarships to college, and the mentor who helped me learn how to organize, manage my time, get internships, and be successful in school—both came after I learned how to forgive myself and let go. I needed someone to address the trauma in my life before I could focus on schoolwork and the pursuits of success that a young person from a functional environment could focus on. I'm convinced that the only reason I met all the people who have helped me in my life and attracted all these opportunities was because I was transformed in the most fundamental way, helping me to change my mentality from the ground up.

What education does not focus on that my mentor addressed so effectively are the challenges and circumstances that impede children's education. If you navigate those issues and help kids understand the complexities of their circumstances and how to deal with distractions in a realistic way, that's really how to create better outcomes.

Kids growing up in extreme poverty are being taught math, history, English, and science at a time when they have real trauma going on in their lives—and then they are expected to be successful. The reality is that most children under these conditions will never be successful—not because they aren't capable of learning but because they haven't recovered from the trauma in their lives. That's why my mentor was so influential in my school. He was one of the rare people who put in the extra effort to ensure that the knowledge we gained in the classroom could be applied in the real world and used to really escape our circumstances. His personal experience with the trauma that most of us were experiencing allowed him to connect with us and to have an informed approach for helping us in the most effective ways.

All those things, combined with a powerful final session that conveyed the message "Let it go. Give it up. Surrender it. Now we're going to begin the process of recovery," really assured that students focused on the important things in life once they let go of what was holding them back.

Mr. McGrone's process was certainly different—radical even—but it was effective. In the inner-city community, educators and social workers don't want kids to be involved with the community, because they perceive it to be corrupt and dangerous—full of thieves, robbers, drug dealers, and dope fiends. The mind-set is that we don't want kids to be involved in that because we want better for them, so we try to shield them from that reality because if we expose them to it, we're going to lose them.

Mr. McGrone was fired from multiple institutions for his unorthodox program and methods. Essentially, many organizations believe that schools should have mentors but that the mentors shouldn't take students outside. They shouldn't take us around to the community to educate us on the conditions of our reality. They shouldn't take us to the liquor store and have us interview the owner to learn how alcohol impacts the community. They shouldn't take us on field trips to a psych ward or a jailhouse. They shouldn't take us to all these places, because they have to play it safe.

We spend so much time trying to shield kids from the reality of life and the reality of their community that we end up hurting them in the long run. From the time they leave their house to the time they get to school, they see it already. They're already exposed to it. Whatever attempts we make to shield kids from the world will only propel them further into it. We must learn to educate them about themselves and their history, rather than try to hide their reality from them.

This is what mentors like mine did. He made it a point to say, "It's not just about you. It's not just about the school. It's about the community. If you don't fix the community, you're never going to fix what's in the school. If you don't fix yourself, you're never going to fix the trajectory of your life. Let's tackle your issues from the deepest, darkest levels. Reconcile those things. Come to terms with those things. Then we can move on to the real business, which is educating you and transforming you into the person you're meant to be. Until we tackle those real, systemic, hard issues that you're dealing with, that you don't tell anybody about, we'll never get anywhere."

Children growing up in crime-ridden communities have likely experienced a great deal of trauma by the time they're thirteen or fourteen years old. From death to physical and sexual abuse to abandonment and neglect, children are exposed to all sorts of traumatic events that have become all too commonplace in their communities. They've seen people who were shot and killed. They know people who were molested. Some of them were molested themselves. They understand the elements of drugs, gangs, and corruption, but we don't have trauma centers in high schools or grade schools to help them process it all.

When we improve education policies in these areas by providing a structure that allows willing leaders to share their knowledge of the students' adversities and how to overcome them, mentors like McGrone can come into our schools, change lives, and make society better as a whole.

Without a far-reaching change in policy, we will continue to see the same frustrating restrictions that Mr. McGrone faced. Prior to becoming a principle, he was fired after one year from almost every institution he had been a part of, as his Renaissance-like thinking was not in line with school policies and guidelines. Most institutions focus on shielding our kids from the community and all of its ills while trying to direct them solely toward college, and that's not going to work. The vast majority of youth won't make a transition out of their community without proper emotional and psychological support.

You'll never see a community of students succeed in an environment that's deprived and at risk until we confront their conditions, which is really what my mentor made a point to do.

CHAPTER SIX

A NEW DAY ONE

We stood in a circle. The fire was blazing, and then streams of ash rose into the air. From that day on, we declared that our adversity would never have power over us again. We freed ourselves from whatever setbacks we experienced, and then we lead new lives.

After the ceremony, I walked home, periodically saying to myself, "What just happened?" I couldn't remember crying like that ever in my life. I was so emotional. I lived in Roseland at the time, on 109th and State. On that day, the bus ride home felt longer than ever.

I sat down outside and cried again that night. For whatever reason, I couldn't stop crying. All the emotions I had suppressed started flowing into my mind all at once. It was a trauma gone untapped for my entire life. I cried about my parents. I cried for my siblings. I cried over how my relationship with my last foster home ended. I cried about my grandmother's passing. I cried for all the things I never cried about. No counselor, social worker, or therapist ever made me feel the way I felt that night.

It was like a wall came down and a flood of emotion poured out of me throughout the night. I wasn't crying out of sadness or despair but rather from a sense of relief and release. For the first time in my life, I felt like I would be able to get out of my pain and struggle. I felt a deep sense of gratitude to Mr. McGrone for helping me shed so much of the emotional stress that I had not been able to release.

Days later, everything started to come full circle for me. Mr. McGrone met up with me, gave me a big hug, and said, "I'm proud you were able to let this stuff go. You've had a hard life. You've really struggled. I saw that struggle from day one. I just wanted to let you know I've never left your side. I never will. I believe that from this day on, you're going to do bigger and better things. Believe me when I tell you that you will share your story with the world and it will save many lives."

I can remember thanking him throughout the day, letting him know how much I appreciated him. That was really where my life took off, in a sense, because I had a changed mind-set from that day on. I was never an angry child. I never lashed out. I never shot anyone. I never fought people. I never cussed anyone out. I never did any of those things, but I was always a child in despair, thinking that my life would inevitably turn out to be some charity case—that I would end up living the same life of poverty and social failure as the people in my community. College never seemed like a viable option, nor did having a successful career. I felt a sense of depravity and despair, believing that I would never live up to my full potential. Before the program, my depression took a very heavy toll.

After the program, I began to wonder how much more I could do. I needed to go further, and I was motivated to see what I could accomplish. I was driven to create a life for myself that would make everyone who ever broke me down look at me and say, "Wow. How did he become that?" That was my goal after that day, and with my ambition renewed and my confidence at an all-time high, I made a promise to myself that I would never go back to my old mind-set.

I knew I needed to orchestrate a vision for myself to show how strong I had become, so I made a "vision board," on which I posted inspiring pictures and words that I wanted in my own life. I would write notes on my notepad to say, "I will be successful. I will be wealthy. I will be prosperous. I will forgive." Another major part of building up this vision for my future stemmed from an activity Mr. McGrone had us do as a part of the Ambassadors program: making a video to our unborn children. I said to my future child, "I just want to let you know that everything is going to be great. I'm going to be wealthy and successful. You're going to come up and have a life much better than mine ever was." All of these activities were to influence my new mentality and inspire it to last.

In my mind, success from that day on was inevitable. Once I discovered that there had to be something more to myself and to life than what I knew, nothing could change the trajectory of my success afterward. I convinced my mind to look for any opportunity that could help make those visions of success a reality. That left me with a tremendous feeling I had never experienced before. After that day, I had hope.

NFTE: THE DOOR
TO DELIVERANCE

Rodney in New York's Times Square, minutes after receiving the second place award for the 2008 NFTE National Entrepreneurship Challenge.

I immediately started looking for opportunities to succeed, and thankfully, I didn't have to search long.

A team from a nonprofit organization came to speak at my school a few weeks later. Calling their organization

NFTE, or the Network for Teaching Entrepreneurship, the group introduced us to the idea of entrepreneurship. "This class is all about entrepreneurship. If you have a passion and you want to find out how to make that passion into a successful business, this is the class for you. This is what you'll be learning throughout this course."

That immediately sparked my interest because at the time, money translated into success in my mind. I thought about my interests and skills, anything that I had ever done or enjoyed that may be useful to the program. I remembered that when I was younger, my brother and I would make music and videos in the basement. We made beats on a computer and rapped over them before making a video to go along with the songs. I developed a passion for video production during that time, but I had largely forgotten about it until I saw NFTE's presentation. I signed up for the class immediately and dove in headfirst, learning as much as I could about building a business plan for the video production company I'd always wanted.

Using a PowerPoint business plan template and the NFTE textbook, our business teacher, Mr. Mercer, taught the curriculum. First we needed to decide what business we would like to create. Then we learned how to create a sales pitch and a mission statement and how to clearly define the product or service we were providing in order to develop the marketing strategy. We learned how to create a competitive advantage, how to find start-up capital, and the ins and outs of fixed cost and all other basic elements of business. After learning these concepts and incorporating them into our PowerPoint, we spent the rest of the semester preparing for citywide and regional student business plan competitions, which would take place at the end of the year.

In the first week of the class, we watched a video of the national business plan competition from the prior year. A Chicago student had won second place in the national competition. I saw his presentation on that video and said to myself, "That's going to be me next year. God willing, when I do this program, I'm going to make it there . . . and I'm going to win that whole competition."

My motivation throughout that year was to work hard preparing my business plan, build relationships with my teachers and my business plan coaches, and master my presentation. Along with NFTE, I also joined Chicago's Future Founders program, spearheaded by Scott Issen. This entrepreneurship program was instrumental in exposing me to entrepreneurs and businesses across the city, polishing my business plan and speaking skills through in-class competitions, and ultimately preparing me for their citywide business plan competition.

Six months later, I won the Future Founders citywide business plan competition. A month after that, I won NFTE's regional business plan competition. Through both the citywide and regional competition, I won more than $5,500. Winning regionals meant that I qualified to compete in NFTE's national business plan competition, set to take place in New York City, in Times Square. Until that point in my life, I had never felt such unimaginable success and motivation. Working so hard on my business plan was easy because I was truly passionate about my idea. And to see the fruits of my hard labor pay off by winning the competition and having the opportunity to represent my city in a national competition was a gratifying experience.

The same year I was in the competition, an independent film production company, 50 Eggs Films, happened to be making a documentary about NFTE and its finalists. Because I was a finalist in that competition, I got to be in the documentary and even ended up serving as the film's narrator. The movie profiled the stories and businesses of the young entrepreneurs in the national competition, showing audiences how NFTE taught kids how to pitch business plans and experience entrepreneurship firsthand. I was elated to be a part of the project because for me it meant that the world would know my journey. While the movie was in development, I was still finishing high school. The national competition wouldn't take place until later that year, in October 2008.

The film production team gave me a video camera to record my life and business experiences leading up to the national competition. The more I thought about the possibility of winning a national competition, or a national anything, the more enthused I became. My life had turned 180 degrees, and the change in my reality seemed surreal to me, as though I was living the life of someone else completely.

KICK-OFF TO COLLEGE

Around the beginning of my senior year in high school, I engaged in serious conversations with my advisory teacher, Ms. Vaughn, about next steps. She approached me with a simple question, for which I had no simple answer. "What are you thinking about for college?" she asked.

At that time, I actually had not thought about college, but I didn't want to disappoint her. "Well, I'm going to apply to a couple of schools because I really want to try to go to college," I said.

After Mr. McGrone's leadership program and the NFTE course, I spent a lot of time thinking about ways I could propel myself to success, and right off the bat, I felt that college was one of those ways. I allowed my mind to focus on that goal and began studying harder. I had a borderline score on the ACT the year prior to that, so all I had to do was apply and write the essays.

My success in the business competitions and my interest in college started to attract a lot of teachers and people who wanted to help me, so I started to stay after school some days to go through the applications with my college counselor.

About a week after winning the regional competition, I received an acceptance letter from Morehouse College, informing me that I'd been admitted on academic probation. In my mind, I felt as if life couldn't get any better. I would have an opportunity of a lifetime to attend one of the top HBCUs in the country. So many exciting things were happening at once, and I was overwhelmed and awestruck with joy and appreciation.

Morehouse College is a prominent institution, and because I was accepted on academic probation, my attendance there came with stipulations. They would offer me no financial aid, and I would have to work my way into the school by getting some decent grades before they could consider me for scholarships.

In my last year of high school, for the first time in my life, I got all As and Bs. I got As in subjects that I had never gotten As in before. After the leadership program and my success through NFTE, I was super focused, ever more determined to get into college. I wanted to make up for the previous years, when I had done so little in school. I made it a point to stay after school to do my homework and talk to the teachers about problems I was having. I joined a couple of extended, after-school classes that provided additional instruction in the subjects with which I struggled.

After my second progress report my senior year, I had all As. I had never achieved academic success like that before, so it proved to me that hard work, confidence, and a sense of self-determination really would create the change I wanted to see. The most amazing feelings are those that we never expect to have, and once I learned how to let go of my fears, pride, and pain, I found all the determination I needed to overcome my adversities. The result was a domino effect of positivity and good fortune. One success led to another, attracting all the right people to my efforts.

MY UNLIKELY MENTORS

NFTE executive director, Christine Poorman, and Rodney at
NFTE National Competition in 2008.
Photo Courtesy of 50 Eggs Films

When I was in NFTE, I always took food home from the events. In the spring semester at a business camp, I was approached by Christine Poorman, who was serving as the executive director of the NFTE program in Chicago. She watched me taking food home a few times at the end of each day of the business camp. Eventually, she approached me, saying, "I've noticed that you're taking food home. Are you sure you don't need a ride home or something? Are you sure you don't need help?"

"No, I'm okay. I got it," I shrugged. "I don't live that far."

I would stuff loads of sandwiches or whatever leftover food was available into my backpack to bring home so that my parents and I could eat. We would find ways to make that food last us for days.

Eventually Christine approached me again and asked more questions about where I lived, what I was going through, where my parents were, what my future plans were, and things like that. I told her, "I'm really hoping to get into college. I haven't gotten an acceptance letter yet, but I want to go to college and get a degree. I want to get a good job or start my own business."

She said, "Well, that's great. What do you think about this business plan course that we're doing?"

I said, "I hope to be successful in that, too. I hope to go to the competition and win the whole thing."

"That's great. We should talk more about it. I see that you always stay late and help us take food home and things like that. Let's talk."

I told her about my situation, that my parents and I were at odds because of their drug addiction, and that I'd been in and out of their house throughout the past year. When she learned the details, she invited me to her house for dinner one night. After that, I began coming over to her house nearly every other week to have dinner with her family. She even started letting me take food home from her house—I would literally take food from her cabinet so that I could go home and fill up my cabinets.

About a week after the citywide business plan competition, I decided I would leave my parents' house entirely at the end of the school year. I reached out to Christine. I said, "I need somewhere to stay for the last couple months before I go to college. I need to be super focused for what I'm trying to do, and I can't get focused at my parents' place. It's too much drama over here." Little did I know that this plea for a better living environment would lead me into another life-changing mentor relationship.

Following the NFTE regional competition, Christine received a call from one of her colleagues at the Chicago Board of Education, a woman named Jane Lee-Kwon. Jane had been at the competition that evening, but she missed my business presentation because of a phone call during the competition. After hearing my story from her boss, who was serving as a judge for the business plan competition, she decided to reach out to Christine for my contact information.

A week after the competition, I received an email from Jane, letting me know that she wanted to meet with me one afternoon for lunch. I emailed her my phone number, and she reached out to me a day later: "Thank you for taking the time to chat. I heard about you and your story. Congratulations on winning the competition. Unfortunately, I didn't get to see your presentation, but my boss told me a little about your business and your story, and I would like to meet you."

A few days later, I went to meet her in downtown Chicago. "I'm glad we had a chance to meet," she said. "Christine spoke so highly of you, and she really believes in you. After my boss told me your story, I felt compelled to reach out to you. I don't know what it was, but I said to myself, 'you gotta meet this kid.' I wanted to talk more about your story and how you got involved with NFTE and find out what you plan to do after school and whether you have any job opportunities lined up for the summer."

"Well, I don't have anything yet, but I'm looking," I said, trying not to appear desperate for a job.

"Well, I can talk to my colleagues at the board of education and see if we can set you up with an interview. Let's follow up and see if we have anything for you."

After our lunch, I thanked her for considering me for an internship. I was really excited about working downtown again, especially at the board of education. I felt it was just what I needed to get focused before starting my journey to college.

PREPARING FOR MOREHOUSE

Rodney and his parents at his high school graduation.

I was living the happiest days of my life up to that point. I knew I was getting away from Chicago and was going to get a fresh start. But before I left, there was one thing I wanted to do more than anything else. I wanted to reunite and organize my family for graduation.

At the time, my siblings were still scattered across Chicago. Some of them I had lost contact with altogether, but one of my biggest goals was to reunite us all. I started calling around to see where they were. I got in touch with all of my brothers and told them, "Hey, I've been cleared for graduation. I hope you can make it out here when I graduate from high school."

Before me, none of my siblings had graduated from high school, so it was a momentous occasion for my parents. One by one, all of my brothers and sisters responded, and we were able to get together in time for my graduation in June. Just to see my family together for that moment was really special for me.

The following month, I landed an internship at the Chicago Board of Education. Through Jane's mentorship, I learned skills and habits that were more valuable than the average student internship. From a professional-development standpoint, my learning curve was steep. I hadn't been equipped with the characteristics and traits of the average young professional because of the environment I was raised in. I was always late to work, and my clothes weren't clean because I had no access to a laundry. I couldn't read my job's correspondence with much proficiency because I couldn't read fast enough. Some days, I would come to work having slept only four hours the night before because I didn't go to sleep early enough. I had no sense of discipline or self-control, because for the most part I had never experienced any real sense of accountability.

Whereas Mr. McGrone helped restore my emotional and psychological health and well-being, Jane equipped me with the hard discipline and accountability that was necessary to be a competent young professional. She held me to a high professional standard as no one had done before. It is very lucky that I'd taken Mr. McGrone's leadership program because without his mentorship, I would have been compelled to do what most poor young men of color would do when confronted with responsibility—get defensive and walk away. But Jane's guidance came into my life at the right time. I was convinced that I needed to turn my life around, and I wanted to be successful, but I needed real help. I needed that person who would yell at me when I showed up late, or when my work wasn't up to par, or when my etiquette and hygiene were poor. I needed someone who would work with me on the practical things, and in this way, Jane was exactly the influence that I needed.

Our mentor/mentee relationship grew beyond the confines of the office. One day, I told Jane that it would help if I had a more stable place to stay. I told her that where I lived, I had no access to a laundry facility, that there was no air conditioning so it was really hard to get a good night's sleep, and that there were too many distractions.

The next day I drove with her from work to her home on the North Side of Chicago, in the West Ridge neighborhood. She let me stay at her place for the rest of the summer, until I left for college. I had never lived in an area like that before, and every time I left work it seemed surreal to me that I was actually going in the right direction.

She bought all my school supplies, my luggage, and my dorm materials. She even bought me new clothes to help with my transition. And perhaps most helpful of all, she helped me find scholarship money through the board of education. She also opened a bank account for me and encouraged her colleagues to give me small checks so that I would have some cash when I got to Atlanta.

Jane Lee-Kwon and Rodney share a goodbye at the Chicago O'Hare Airport minutes before leaving for Atlanta's Morehouse College in August 2008. It was Rodney's first flight.

On August 18, 2008, four days after my nineteenth birthday, Jane drove me to my very first flight out of Chicago and saw me off to Atlanta. I didn't get much sleep the night before, as my heart was racing with anticipation. In the days leading up to the move, I was staying with Jane and her husband, John, and we did all the shopping and packing needed in preparation for my departure. After checking in for my flight at O'Hare, Jane and I exchanged some final words. "Well, my son, this is where we part," she said. "I'm so proud of how far you've come, and I know you're going to do great. You know that John and I are a phone call away if you ever need anything. Call me when you land. Love you." To this day, I consider her my "Korean mom." She did more for me than I can ever repay.

CHAPTER SEVEN

LEARNING TO WALK AGAIN

M r. McGrone, Jane, and Christine were critical to my success during my first two years at Morehouse. When I came to college, I was at a disadvantage because there was a lot of material I didn't understand. I started out at a very basic level in reading and math, as I had missed so much of that focus in high school. There were times when I was really discouraged and needed motivation. Thankfully, my mentors always put a good word in my ear and gave me a lot of wisdom and encouragement. They affirmed my destiny for success in a lot of ways.

Every time I came home, whether in the summer, winter, or spring, they always made sure I had a place to stay if I had nowhere else to go. For the first couple of years, I would shift back and forth to my family's place, but for the most part I stayed at Jane's house on the North Side when I was home.

I would spend weeks there before returning to school, and she would take me shopping to get school clothes, job uniforms, toiletries, and things that I needed back in Atlanta. She and her husband would take me out to eat, and in many ways they were really like my parents away from home.

They constantly reinforced how important it was that I was in college and made sure that I was successful in my internships. They always assured me that whatever I needed, they would be there to support me in whatever way they could.

Christine was also very influential. She made sure I was looking into opportunities to speak with other young people about why they should go to college and how important it was for them to find a mentor. Not only did she make sure I had a place to stay, but her children became like brothers and sisters to me. Being a part of her world opened my mind up further and exposed me to a lifestyle that most people in my Englewood and Roseland communities will never experience. I felt like I was on a completely different planet. Her neighborhood, family, and community dynamic gave more substance to my vision of the life I wanted.

Christine also made sure that I had opportunities through NFTE, whether internships, speaking opportunities, or anything else that would help me succeed. She was always there for me, and she continues to be a pivotal person in my life.

Last, but certainly not least, was Mr. McGrone's support during my Morehouse years. He was the mentor who really changed things for me from the inside out because I would often call him from school and let him know that I had final exams coming up and how frustrated I was about not understanding the material. He would share some wisdom and insight about how he went through the same struggles in college. He would motivate me by telling me to see it through. "Always ask questions. Don't be too proud to ask for help," he would tell me. He really made sure I had the right mind-set for a lot of those obstacles in college.

LIKE-MINDED LEADERSHIP

My mentors were in my circle on a daily basis, encouraging me to persevere through college, and whatever I needed they were there for me. Their support was one of two major factors in my college success. The second factor was my involvement with the Institute for Responsible Citizenship, an organization that brings together some of the most intelligent, accomplished African American young men for a two-summer leadership program, starting in the summer after sophomore year. The goal is to prepare young, talented men to be great citizens and leaders of our country and the world. In many ways this organization affected just how far I would go after Morehouse. When I joined the organization at the end of my sophomore year, I was suddenly connected with a network of successful, promising African American men of my age with very inspiring backgrounds and from many different institutions.

As a group, the energy we felt around each other, the brainstorming that occurred naturally as we interacted on a daily basis, and the conversations that we had all magnified the inspiration we felt from being around one another and fueled our desire to be more successful. For me, that inspiration and being in that kind of network with that circle of people really motivated me to persevere.

My support system at Morehouse was also greatly impacted by my continuing to stay in touch with NFTE. The program technically ended for me in my senior year of high school, but I had met so many influential people through the organization, and they provided me with opportunities I could not otherwise have even imagined.

Through NFTE, I had the chance to go to Monte Carlo during my sophomore year for the Ernst and Young Entrepreneur of the Year awards. I had never been out of the country before, but I'd always imagined what it would be like to be on a yacht in France. I stayed in a five-star hotel, and along with the other entrepreneurs who were there, I got to share in some of life's luxuries.

Imagine the impact that this exposure could have on the minds of young people who every day see only poverty and homelessness. Here I was, a young entrepreneur aspiring to be successful, with a large group of internationally acclaimed entrepreneurs around me. The experience was a very big deal for me, and I continue to draw inspiration from it for my efforts today.

Yet another critical key to success came into focus after that trip—the power of networking. Engaging with a network that exposed me to the global business community and the opportunities such a community presents was pivotal to my success. If I could name just one factor, a healthy network was the biggest asset that NFTE provided me, and it is critical to this day.

When I returned to the States, I was more motivated than ever. I had a taste of international travel and a clearer vision for the type of success I wanted for myself. My motivation turned to a sudden rush of excitement when I received a call informing me that the documentary I had taken part in several months before was a success. The national education documentary *Ten9Eight: Shoot for the Moon* was set to release, and I was invited to a special screening at the Aspen Film Festival in Colorado.

I was thrilled to attend and get a chance to see the work on screen, but I was also looking forward to spending time with supporters and mentors both inside and outside the NFTE program. I reconnected with Arne Duncan, whom I had gotten to know while interning at the Chicago Board of Education a couple years before and who had recently been appointed the US secretary of education.

After the screening, I was invited to a large dinner party, where I sat with a table of familiar and unfamiliar faces making conversation about the documentary and about my journey before and after it was filmed. I had been introduced to a woman at the table named Patty Alper earlier in the day, and while I could never have foreseen it back then, today she has become a truly great mentor to me. Based in Maryland, Patty has her own foundation and serves as a board member for NFTE, and she was instrumental in getting the film featured at the Aspen Film Festival. Patty invited me to have lunch with her and her colleagues the afternoon of the screening. All throughout the day, I'd felt out of my element. I was surrounded by a group of affluent businessmen and businesswomen, and it was really socially awkward for me. So I was excited and grateful to be approached by Patty and be taken around to network with the community.

Our afternoon lunch conversation with her friends and colleagues soon turned to Morehouse and my experience as a first-generation college student. "I feel privileged to be there," I told them. As we talked about Morehouse, the conversation eventually began to focus on the fact that, financially, I was having some problems with my college education. "Tuition is very expensive at Morehouse. I, um . . . I just don't have the money to continue pursuing my degree, unless I continue looking for loans. My grades were so poor in high school that I was ineligible for scholarships when I got there. But last year I made a 3.5 GPA, and I've been working hard despite my financial troubles. I believe my education will lead to something great."

And right then, without any hesitation, a lady at the table said, "Let me know what you need. I'll pay for the remainder of your time there."

At first I was confused and at a loss for words. I didn't know what she meant. Pay for the rest of my college? It seemed too crazy to be real, and I thought I had misheard her.

"Really?" I stammered, a kind of reflex in the absence of thought and words.

She smiled and said again, "I'll pay for your expenses. Just let me know how much you need each semester. Write up a proposal, and I'll send you a check."

She was so matter-of-fact and nonchalant that the extent of what she was offering took several minutes to sink in, and even then I couldn't believe what was happening. We set up an agreement that the money would be handled like a trust by NFTE, who would give me the funds I needed each year to cover my tuition and fees. Patty was the driving force of that relationship, and because of her, I was able to stay in school.

Patty was also the reason I was able to meet some very important people who really shaped the opportunities I received well after our first meeting. Every time I go to Washington, D.C., for anything, I make sure to get in touch with Patty and let her know how thankful I am. She was the mentor I really needed at that time in my life; she exposed me to the business community and other opportunities for growth and development that I would likely never have received otherwise, and she is still a great mentor of mine.

SPEAKING TO THE POWERS OF CHANGE

Rodney delivering his keynote to MasterCard Corporation's leadership team at its 2013 leadership conference in Key Biscayne, Florida.

I returned to Morehouse feeling weightless, finally freed of much of the worry that had burdened me during my freshman and sophomore years. NFTE remained in touch after Aspen as well, having requested that I speak at a number of fundraisers throughout my junior and senior years. I would have an opportunity to tell my story at galas, events, and competitions, building my speaking skills and validating NFTE's work at the same time.

NFTE would contact me throughout the year from time to time and let me know when there was an opportunity to speak or be a part of an initiative and meet some great people or advocate on behalf of their programs. Over the years, I got to attend so many events and meet a lot of fascinating people, such as Chris Gardner, the author of *The Pursuit of*

Happyness, and Chelsea Clinton, both of whom I still keep in touch with.

I was able to advocate in a number of different news outlets about NFTE, recounting how they helped me get the skills and resources I needed to be successful. They were instrumental in providing me with the support and resources necessary for my rise out of poverty, so it was great to be able to give a little back.

But public speaking didn't come easily to me. NFTE would send me to events where I would speak before hundreds of people, which completely terrified me in the beginning. I was a good speaker, but I was shy by nature and had never been comfortable with speaking in public. I had intensive stage fright and was overcome with nerves every time I spoke. I was afraid of messing up or coming off the wrong way, and I often swelled with fear that I would embarrass myself by tripping on the stage or throwing up mid-speech.

I can still remember the first big speech I gave, at the national business plan competition for NFTE in October of 2010. The event brings the top thirty-five students from around the country to New York City to present their business plans. I had presented at the competition in high school, but this year I was the keynote speaker.

With hundreds of people in attendance, I was so worried about throwing up that I wouldn't eat before I spoke. I remember squeezing my eyes shut and taking as many deep breaths as I could while time inched by, waiting for my announcement.

When they introduced me, all I can remember is a spotlight that beamed on me so bright I couldn't see the audience. I remember a sense of relief that I couldn't see anybody, but that didn't calm my nerves. But I knew the fear came from being exposed to something for the first time, and that I just needed to get used to it.

I stumbled as I started to speak. I didn't actually know everything I was going to say. I read off of a note card for the first two minutes or so, trembling as I spoke my first few sentences. But then I got more comfortable and started walking the stage and telling my story, telling the audience what a great impact NFTE had on me and how I was able to use what this organization did to influence and inspire my growth and development.

I remember that day clearly. Such great stress and great relief. When I finished my speech, I got a standing ovation. I remember being filled with an incredible feeling and saying to myself, "Wow, I really touched lives today. I really did a good thing."

After I got off stage, several people came up to me and told me what a good job I'd done. They told me they loved how I was a survivor and said I needed to tell my story to more people. I got a lot of business cards from people asking me to speak to their kids, organizations, initiatives, fundraisers, and more.

I was so fearful of speaking that I didn't really consider the offers. But the more I spoke for NFTE, the better I got, the more polished I got, and the better I was at navigating an audience. I learned how to steer the feelings and thoughts of an audience in a way that I hadn't known was possible prior to these engagements. Over time, I started to wonder if speaking and mentoring was what I was born to do—a thought I would never have had if NFTE hadn't provided me with the opportunities to tell my story and to really hone in on that hidden skill.

All these opportunities came to me at once after that speech, which was baffling to me because I didn't think I had done all that well. But after that moment, it was on. I had speaking engagements all over the country and in Europe, at various events and schools.

It started to feel like I was leading two different lives. One week I would be traveling, eating food I'd never heard of at fancy galas and restaurants and rubbing elbows with very successful people, and the next week I'd be back in South Side or Atlanta, walking around streets with homeless people and families just scraping by. Keeping myself balanced was critical to me, as I didn't want to forget where I came from any more than I wanted to forget where I could go.

CHAPTER
EIGHT

ROAD TO YALE

When I first got to Morehouse, I had no real concept of what college was about. Most people who go to college have an idea of what they want to be and how they're going to get there. They use college as a vehicle to get where they want to go, but I was just using college as a means to be successful, without any specific career in mind. In other words, I didn't come to college and say, "I want to be this major. I want to take these types of classes. I want to do this type of work. This is how I'm going to do it." I had no vision of that.

When I got to college and learned I had to pick a major, my first thought was, "What's a major? What does that mean?" My advisors explained that a major is an area of focus, but I had no idea what I wanted to do. I just knew I wanted to be the first person in my family to graduate from college.

I had no strategy, no vision for how I was going to use the college experience for my overall success in life, so I struggled with choosing classes strategically that oriented me toward my success. When my advisor asked me what I wanted to be, I explained, "I like debating. I like critical thinking. I like to study the mind. I like how you can dream about something or visualize something and it can come true if you work hard and keep it in your mind. I want to go into a major that talks about that."

He said, "Psychology or philosophy would be best for that."

"I'd like to do both then." And that was it. I was a philosophy major and a psychology minor from that day on.

I enrolled in classes on philosophical thinking and learned about the great ideas of Socrates, Spinoza, Hegel, St. Augustine, and many other great thinkers throughout history. I wasn't sure I'd actually be interested in philosophy, but through my studies I really developed a serious interest, and that made me want to go further. Throughout my time in college, I studied great thinkers, learning how they thought and how they attracted people to their ideas.

I wrote about how I could translate that into my community and how deep thinking combined with a vision could affect the African American community and people of color. I wanted to understand how this knowledge could be used to influence change, and that is where I focused my college studies. By my senior year at Morehouse, I wanted to take my ideas further, to educate people on the workings of the mind and how proper education, through the lens of enlightened thinking, can influence and change communities.

Through my membership in the Institute for Responsible Citizenship, I met Rhodes Scholars and Truman Scholars and interacted with people who went to top-tier schools and represented the best in their class. Going into my senior year, I had a conversation with one institute scholar named Elijah Heyward, who was a graduate of Yale Divinity School. He said, "I know you're studying philosophy and ethics. I graduated from Yale Divinity School, and they have a great program there if you're interested. If you want me to get you in touch with the admissions there, let me know."

I didn't have to think about his offer long, replying almost immediately that I wanted to apply. I told him that I wanted to focus on how philosophy and philosophical ethics can influence change in the African American community and how ministry can influence people's emotions and spirit as we try to transform communities. Elijah mentored me through the process of applying, and about three months after I applied to Yale, I was accepted.

Getting an acceptance letter from a school like Yale was a momentous event for me. It surprised my friends and colleagues at Morehouse and NFTE, but it amazed everyone back home. When I called my mother to deliver the news, she sat silently on the other end for a few seconds before she said, "Yale? What . . . wow, that's great news!"

"I'm very excited," I told her. "I can't wait to come home. We're going to celebrate." She laughed with joy for a few seconds, which was the best response I could have asked for.

A few months later, I graduated from Morehouse College, and Mr. McGrone, Jane, and Christine

Mr. McGrone congratulates Rodney after the Morehouse commencement ceremonies in 2008.

Jane Lee-Kwon and Christine Poorman traveled to Atlanta to watch Rodney's graduation from Morehouse.

all came down to Atlanta. I can remember Mr. McGrone telling me, "I'm proud of you. I'm glad about your next journey. Again, this isn't even the tip of the iceberg, but I can see what's ahead because I know it's going to be great."

Christine and Jane also told me how proud and excited they were to see me going so far, and it was a truly great event that I'll never forget.

WELCOME TO YALE

When I first stepped foot on Yale's campus, I was amazed that I was even there. Just seeing the historic buildings and a sign that read "Welcome to Yale University" left me awestruck.

The grass, the trees, the buildings, the architecture, and the history—altogether, the campus made me feel like I'd been transported to a different time, a long-preserved intellectual past with overtones of American regality, which now was open to me. I remember thinking, "Whoa, this is really me. I'm really here." And while much of the New Haven area around Yale was riddled with the same type of poverty found on the South Side, the campus itself was a completely different atmosphere from anything I had ever seen before. I kept reminding myself how privileged I was, taking moments to collect my thoughts before saying over and over to myself, "So many people apply to Yale and would die for this opportunity. I can't believe I'm really in this class . . . with these like-minded scholars . . . at this institution." It took me a couple days to understand what I had done, to get over that awestruck feeling of being there. That's when the real work began.

When I started classes, I realized quickly that it was going to be a difficult adjustment. I couldn't even understand the professors' speech patterns and instruction styles. As a result, I didn't comprehend a lot of the material, but the classes were interesting to me all the same.

I had papers to write and frequent exams, but in the beginning it felt like I was on a steep learning curve, especially when it came to writing papers. Although I had graduated from Morehouse and had written many papers there, I felt like my level of writing was not where it should have been. So I went back to what I knew best: I called my mentors for words of encouragement and advice.

Too many people feel that they're inconveniencing people when they ask for help, or they simply have too much pride to ask. It takes a certain level of humility to ask for help, and you have to have that and exercise it to make sure you get the help you need to be successful. A positive aspect of my circumstances growing up was that I learned at an early age that when I needed something, I had to speak up. I continued that practice throughout my college experience and into my present life.

Yale offered writing consultants that I could go to during the school year. Because of the abundant resources that Yale had to offer, I never felt alone. Help was always literally around the corner, so I never felt like I was at a disadvantage. After a few months, my writing had improved, my ability to understand my professors had grown, and I was adjusting to my overall academic workload quite well.

Most of my time at Yale was spent between the classroom at the school and the basketball court at the gym. Every other day, I would play basketball as an outlet for my worries and nervous energy. Whenever school stressed me out, I would go to the Payne Whitney gym and play pick-up games. The stress built quickly and steadily, and I ended up playing an average of five basketball games every day during the majority of my time at Yale.

Even though it was a privilege and an honor to be at Yale, I struggled socially in many ways. My experiences growing up were so different from the majority of people at Yale that I felt a little isolated from the other students. When I was at Morehouse, most students I knew had experience with inner-city at-risk neighborhoods, so it made talking about it easier. At Yale, I could not find a group that I could socialize with and just be at one with, and that created a lot of isolation and socially awkwardness for me. My conversations with people were very short-winded, not lasting more than a few minutes. I did find some great people and made some great friends who I still keep in touch with, but there was an inevitable cultural struggle. Fortunately, I joined a support group at the school during my first year, and there I had the chance to befriend very talented people who shared my enthusiasm for community and social support. This group, which started as a bible study group, became for me the perfect example of the community that I would like to have throughout my life. We were all seminary students, with different backgrounds and perspectives, and our conversations about the Bible, faith, and world events were rich and full of wisdom.

My area of focus at Yale really had an emphasis on two areas: financial literacy and economic empowerment in poor, at-risk communities; and how faith-based organizations in the black community can reclaim their position as beacons of hope and change in their respective communities. So while I was there, I studied how the black church influenced the Civil Rights movement and the ministry and how the ministry influenced not only black American culture but also the culture of the oppressed in general—of all people living in poverty.

I also studied how the black church was instrumental in influencing our policies, our decisions, and our culture, as well as how the black community has done over time with that influence. And finally, I studied what the black church means to the community today and how relevant it is in today's society, examining whether it makes a meaningful difference. That focus on at-risk communities and the oppressed from the graduate level at Yale propelled my learning and overall experience to heights I had never imagined.

As a child, because I switched foster homes so often, I'd never been able to be part of a church community, and I'd never really had an allegiance—an affiliation with any denomination or church. But while I'd never had that experience, I'd always had a belief in God and that there was something greater than man orchestrating the fortunes and misfortunes of this world.

I struggled with how to believe in God throughout much of my youth because I was never part of a community of believers. I grew up in foster homes with Christians and with nonbelievers, but most of the time when I got into conversations about God, it was always more intellectual than spiritual. It was really hard to have conversations where

I could come to a conclusion about God and how to believe. But the gravity of being in a Yale graduate program centered on theology encouraged me to seek a church community of my own.

Dr. Frederick Streets, the former chaplain at Yale and a great professor during my time there, really helped me spearhead my academic focus on African American churches and their role in serving as centers for healing in trauma-filled communities. Out of that spiritual urge, I began attending church in New Haven at Dr. Streets's church, Dixwell Avenue Congregational Church, the oldest African American Congregational Church in the world. It was there, in that church, that I formed a deeper bond with a spiritual community and a greater mentor/mentee relationship with Dr. Streets.

I soon became a member, and just receiving the word every Sunday rejuvenated my spirit after a long week of studies wore me down. That community support and the wisdom and guidance I found in the services made the transition into graduate life easier in more ways than I can say. I'd never had that before arriving in New Haven, because church had never been an integral part of my life. It was only from my experience with Dr. Streets and his congregation that I first felt the meaning of church, which is simply to provide people with an outlet and offer a place of peace and spiritual relief. In that way, the church grew on me, helping me to see the importance of meditation and spirituality to guide my life choices.

Today, meditation and prayer have become an ongoing practice for me. They are not something I was born with. To me, meditation and prayer are deliberate acts of the mind, for when you've brought yourself to a place of discipline where you know you want to achieve something, but you have to get to a point where you can see it and feel it first. In my experience, I find that it's important to meditate, reflect, and pray over those things on a consistent basis until I get to that point. Once I learned the power of my mind and the sheer force of visualization, my life made sense to me. All I had to do was follow my mind's vision for my life.

A SHORT WALK FOR
A LONG SHOT

After being cleared for graduation a couple weeks prior, my anticipation was rising rapidly. I became more reflective, and feelings of overwhelming joy became more prevalent. In a matter of days, I—a quiet kid from South Side's underbelly—would follow the footsteps of so many prestigious minds and claim a Yale degree of my own.

Just the thought of my family all leaving the only thing they knew in Chicago, to visit one of many worlds that I'd been a part of, felt extremely rewarding. My parents called every other day to let me know how proud they were and how they couldn't wait to see me on graduation day. My closest mentors consistently reaffirmed me and let me know this was an occasion they would not miss. The closer I got to the day, the more I started to think, "This is real. This is actually happening to me, to my family, to South Side, to everyone who struggles to believe in the impossible." I felt the presence of everything the moment represented apart from me. It was a feeling that I can only describe as otherworldly—a fulfillment of dreams on behalf of so many—that resonated deep within.

On the morning of May 19, I woke up feeling like I hadn't gotten a full night's sleep. I hadn't been able to sleep, with so much excitement racing through my body. All night I'd closed my eyes and recapped my entire life experience. I thought about all the heartbreak and agony I went through in foster care. I thought about the depression I felt from missing an entire childhood with my siblings. I thought about my struggles in school and my days in special education classes. I thought about the days I spent isolated from the world, feeling hopeless and distraught. I thought about the days I asked myself, "What is all this for? God, what do you have going on up there? I don't understand all of this, but I know that you do. Please help me find my way."

The line for the commencement ceremony stretched a few blocks down Prospect Street toward the main campus. We listened to the college president's remarks and the faculty acknowledging the various colleges at the university. I found my parents and mentors in the audience, all of them smiling wide and applauding.

Afterward, the graduating class and I walked back to the divinity school campus, where we received our degrees.

I shared the common feeling of having graduated from one of the top universities in the world. Parents and family were overjoyed, and graduate students were overwhelmed to have finally completed the long journey. I gathered for pictures with my family, socialized with other graduates, and truly enjoyed the moment of having achieved such an improbable accomplishment.

Rodney receives his Master's diploma at the Yale commencement ceremonies in May 2014.

CONCLUSION

$\mathbf{A}$fter my graduation from Yale, I moved back to Atlanta and landed my first job in finance at an industrial supply company. I remember walking into my first apartment and looking around the living room at stacks upon stacks of boxes. I felt that my life had come full circle, a complete metamorphosis from where I had begun, and now I was pointed in a direction I would never have thought possible less than ten years before. I began opening boxes and looking over papers that I'd received from the Midwest Adoption Center, until something caught my attention. One of the papers was from a medical center discussing autism. I read closer and realized that it was a test result, diagnosing me with autism.

When I was younger, I was in school for special education. I came into kindergarten in special education because I was diagnosed as a child with special needs. I didn't understand what those special needs were until that moment. As it turns out, I had been diagnosed with autism when I was five years old, and my parents had been told that I was mildly retarded. I was put in special education classes by the Department of Children and Family Services throughout grade school because, according to my teachers, I wasn't reading and writing at grade level.

On a personality scale, I was very introverted. I was reserved and struggled to fit in with the rest of the student population. They didn't give me medication for autism, but they did put me in therapy and counseling to try to rectify it.

Had I discovered this file before my journey, I don't think it would have ever started. I just couldn't have weathered any more challenges or insecurities. But reading that document with my Yale degree on the wall of my new apartment, in a great city with a great job, only helped me understand why humility is so important and why I've got to let that old stuff go. The things of the past happened, and I have to make peace with them and move on with my life. *I have made something of my life,* I thought, *because I am destined for greatness.*

By the time I read that diagnosis, it was just something to marvel over. To me, it only added to the depths of where I was back then and made me feel that much more blessed to be where I am now. That moment, when I read about my learning disabilities, was a moment of pure gratitude. Thankfully, I found out at a perfect time, as I was on an all-time high and felt that nothing would stop me.

If you tell a kid something about himself or herself and keep hammering it into their mind, eventually they will dictate their reality based on that affirmation. Choose your affirmations to be positive. Continued negative affirmations would have defined my reality in a very different way. In my case, it was a good thing that I was so naive, oblivious, and blind to any further discouragement because I probably would have had a much different outcome in life.

After I read my papers, I realized that it was love that really saved me from a life of despair and failure and propelled me into a life of success. Of all the things that happened to me in my early life that contributed to me overcoming my obstacles and my adversity, it was the unconditional love and support from others. My mentors did not have to do what they did. They did it out of love. And what Mr. McGrone did in particular—that was an act of love.

To imagine all the things he sacrificed to make sure I was successful and that I recovered astounds me. He had so much love for the people he was doing this work for that he sacrificed a thirteen-year relationship with his wife for the sake of making sure we were okay. He made sure that I and the other young men and women in his program knew that we were cared for and that our lives mattered.

I'll never forget the incredible sacrifice he made. He could have easily just said, "I want to do this program after school from four to six, and then I'm going to go home. I'm going to get a paycheck. That's it." Instead, he really saw to it that he did whatever he could to make sure we understood our own value and our own worth.

I didn't understand the value of self-love until somebody else loved me that strongly and sincerely. I can't truly say that I loved and cared about myself before then. I needed a real father figure to tell me, "Your life matters. I want you to know that. If there's anything I can do to make sure you realize that, I will do it."

For anyone hoping to ascend from poverty and rise into a functional life, you must begin with a sense of affirmation. You have no idea what is coming. You must believe that it will be good. I tell young people that you really have to bring yourself to believe that the best is yet to come and that you haven't even reached the tip of the iceberg. I explain to them that there are things coming that they can't possibly see yet, but if anyone puts their mind in the right position to experience success, their dreams will come true. Understandably, we need strong role models, and in some cases, we need an entire community to help us achieve this mind-set.

We all want the same things. We all want security. We all want to be economically empowered. We all want love. We want the things we all desire in life, but only a few of us are shown the way to them. As young people, the fact that we have to grow up so fast and navigate our life on our own is not fair, but this is the reality for a lot of youth around the country.

For anyone in struggle, take this day forward as a new day one—as a new stepping-stone to greater things—by letting go. Forgive. Forgive yourself and others to free yourself from your old life and give yourself a new beginning.

Whatever decisions or mistakes you have made up until now, you can let them go. Know that great opportunities for a successful life are just around the corner if you can follow the principles of affirmation and great vision, and allow yourself to receive guidance and wisdom from others. Decipher the positive things about my life experience and how I've used my life as a living example of the greater things to come. You are worth more than your past. Now it's up to you to determine your own value.

No one can go back and make a new beginning,
but anyone can start today and make a new ending. . . .

CHAPTER REFLECTIONS

_____

_____

_____

_____

_____

_____

_____

_____

_____

_____

_____

_____

_____

_____

_____

_____

CHAPTER REFLECTIONS

151

APPENDIX

I n the process of writing this educational memoir, which has been a span of the last three to four years, there have been various works of literature, media, and support from organizations that have deeply influenced and navigated the direction of my life and the culmination of this book. These entities have enlightened and inspired my life's trajectory, and I use these resources as guidance, wisdom, and motivation in my pursuit of a virtuous and meaningful life. I encourage you to further explore these references, for I sincerely believe that they all have the potential to be the life-changing difference that you've been waiting for.

BOOKS:

The Secret by Rhonda Byrne
The Power of Your Subconscious Mind by Joseph Murphy
The Other Wes Moore by Wes Moore
Breaking Night: A Memoir of Forgiveness, Survival, and My Journey from Homeless to Harvard by Liz Murray
The Souls of Black Folk by W. E. B. Du Bois
Rich Dad, Poor Dad by Robert T. Kiyosaki
Think and Grow Rich by Napoleon Hill

*The New Jim Crow: Mass Incarceration in the Age of
Colorblindness* by Michelle Alexander
Invisible Man by Ralph Ellison
How to Win Friends and Influence People by Dale Carnegie
Mindset by Carol Dweck
Become Your Own Boss in 12 Months by Melinda F. Emerson
The Power of Now by Eckhart Tolle
Crisis in the Village by Dr. Robert Franklin
*Who Owns the Icehouse? Eight Life Lessons from an Unlikely
Entrepreneur* by Clifton Taulbert and Gary Schoeniger

MOVIES/FILMS:

The Pursuit of Happyness
The House I Live In
Waiting for Superman
Good Will Hunting
Ten9Eight: Shoot for the Moon

ORGANIZATIONS:

The Institute for Responsible Citizenship
  https://theinstitute.net
The Network for Teaching Entrepreneurship
  www.nfte.com
Youth Guidance
  www.youth-guidance.org

College Possible
   www.collegepossible.org
Mentoring Tomorrow's Leaders (MTL)
Advantage Media Group
   www.advantagefamily.com
The Entrepreneurial Learning Initiative
   https://elimindset.com